Bryn

SHOOTING TYPES

GILES CATCHPOLE & BRYN PARRY

Happy shooting!

Bryn

SWAN·HILL

PRESS

Copyright © 2003 Giles Catchpole (Text) and Bryn Parry (Illustrations)
First published in the UK in 2003 by Swan Hill Press, an imprint of Quiller Publishing Ltd.

British Library Cataloguing-in-Publication Data
A catalogue record for this book
is available from the British Library

ISBN 1 904057 29 2

Typeset and produced by **think : graphic design**, Ludlow, England
Printed in Hong Kong

Swan Hill Press
an imprint of Quiller Publishing Ltd.
Wykey House, Wykey, Shrewsbury, SY4 1JA, England
Tel: 01939 261616 Fax: 01939 261606
E-mail: info@quillerbooks.com
Website: www.swanhillbooks.com

SHOOTING TYPES
GILES CATCHPOLE & BRYN PARRY

CONTENTS

ACKNOWLEDGEMENTS

Our thanks are largely due to Mike Barnes, editor and publisher of The Shooting Gazette, who originally proposed the Shooting Types column to us and insisted we get together to do it.

Mike Beach has long been a staunch supporter of Bryn's and has probably the largest collection of original Shooting Types in private hands in the world. Thanks are due also to all those kind people who still invite us shooting and who keep and beat and pick-up after us and who are all very special Types indeed.

Giles Catchpole & Bryn Parry

Foreword

by the Earl of Leicester

PRUDENS QUI PATIENS

Holkham Hall has long been associated with game shooting and my illustrious forbear Thomas William Coke – Coke of Norfolk – may be said to have contributed materially to the development of driven shooting as we know it today. The Game Books here record every day's shooting on the estate since 1793 and over the past 200-odd years any number of guests have shot here. It is reasonable to assume that among their number there have been a wide variety of shooting types, from hardened tyros to nervous novices; from the finest game Shots in England to the most dangerous Guns in the Empire. Admiral Lord Nelson, who was born nearby at Burnham Thorpe, was notorious apparently for walking all day with his muzzleloader at full cock but then he was equally well known for being ready to engage the enemy at all times.

Over the past few years Giles Catchpole and Bryn Parry have been diligently observing Guns, beaters, keepers, pickers-up and the full supporting panoply and cast at shoots formal and informal up and down the country and bravely displaying them in their Shooting Types column in The Shooting Gazette. Now they have collected them together in this splendidly funny book and added a whole raft of new types for good measure.

Anyone who shoots or beats or picks-up will immediately recognise friends and acquaintances among their number and all will stand in awe of Mrs Judge and remember with a shudder the Dangerous Gun. I think we all know some of these dogs too.

Whether readers will be able to spot themselves within these pages is another question altogether; for it is never easy to see ourselves as others see us. I am confident however that I am not included; first because I am not even slightly like any of these Types; secondly because Giles and Bryn wouldn't have asked me to write this foreword if they were going to lampoon me only a few pages later; and mostly because they both know that if I am on display here they will never be invited to shoot at Holkham again.

Edward Leicester

Leicester
Holkham Hall 2003

THE WET WEATHER WARRIOR

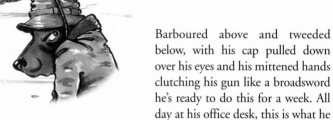

January. The wind is a pure easterly. There is nothing between here and the Siberian steppe except Norway and Norway isn't exactly a bed of roses at this time of year, saunas notwithstanding. What they call in Norfolk a lazy wind. "Tha' dun't go roun' yew; blas', she jes' gew threw." Cruel. It is fronted by a bitter sleet which is not unlike having red hot needles fired into your face at close range. At least it did while there was sensation enough to feel it. Even the spaniels are hiding behind their master's legs. Fillings ache. Bugger Botox, if you want your eyebrows paralysed, try facing this breeze for five minutes.

The plough underfoot is claggy. Three steps and each boot is carrying a slab of brown concrete that forces the feet apart and makes progress look like that of a deep sea diver plodding along the rim of the Atlantic shelf. Slow, measured steps. Toes frozen by icy ground. Agonising. Each foot must be carefully levered free of the infernal sod if boot and foot are to remain in contact. On, on you noblest of Romans! At least no one has been foolish enough to direct more than a glance at the hares scampering hither and yon along the furrows.

In the middle distance is a pit full of elder which may, might, must contain a pheasant which could, should just make this whole miserable trek worthwhile. No, not worthwhile, but justifiable. Almost. "Gentlemen in England now abed will laugh themselves stupid and think themselves bloody lucky they were not here!" Breakfast and a lean against the Aga is a remote memory. Lunch and the dining room fire but a distant hope.

And the Wet Weather Warrior is just lapping it up.

Barboured above and tweeded below, with his cap pulled down over his eyes and his mittened hands clutching his gun like a broadsword he's ready to do this for a week. All day at his office desk, this is what he thinks about. Staring at his computer screen, this is what he sees. Nature red in tooth and claw. Basic. Fundamental. The other Guns would go along with the mental, but the fun part went out of this the moment they stepped out of the front door. He won't be stopped though. "Time for a couple more drives before lunch, then?" His dog stands whimpering behind him in the gale, wondering how to pronounce "Strike!" in human. His wife, - "Come on, old girl, bit of a blow. Do you good! Stroll in the park." - is rehearsing a telephone call to her solicitor. "Cruelty" is a good word. "Anguish" is another.

"Do you know" yells the WWW, genuinely perplexed, above the howl of the wind "that there are actually people who have been camping outside Harrods for days and nights to save a few quid on a new telly? Now, just how damn silly an idea is that, I ask you? They need their heads examining, if you ask me."

The other Guns do not ask him. Their lips are frozen.

"What say we look in at the pond on the Old Spinney before elevenses?" says the WWW with a gleam in his eye, "There may a duck about in this weather, and they wouldn't half go on this breeze. Only take us twenty minutes. Come on!" And he's off across the plough before frozen fingers have fumbled a safety catch to shoot him where he stands. He is the Wet Weather Warrior. There is nothing to stop him. Oh well, on we go.

THE MAGNET

It's just a coincidence to start with. It must be. There is no such thing as a pheasant magnet. Just like there is no truth in the rumour that salmon prefer women. It's just that women catch more and bigger fish than men and some Guns are always under the pheasants. Perhaps it is just because they are especially good shots and therefore seldom let a chance pass without making an impression. Or perhaps it is because wherever they are they still get more chances than they have any right to, and then seldom let them pass without making an impression. Stick them round the back out of the way? Just a couple of brace. Walking Gun on the upwind side of a shelter belt in a howling gale? Marvellous drive. Can't think why they all came out the side door. Locked inside the lunch hut? Just managed to slip out of the window as the birds came through.

It would be better if he was somehow objectionable. Cruel and uncharitable and brazenly immodest. Then at least one would have a sensible and sportsmanlike reason for these dark feelings of hostility. But he is so resolutely charming and ineffably modest that is impossible to harbour misgivings for long. Then you stick him up the side of a hedge, well out of the way, and he's having the shoot of the decade.

Wild birds you could almost understand. Wild birds are flighty and unpredictable and cannot be relied upon to follow any sort of regular course. Then again the wild bird is supposed to be crafty enough to pick up the vibe from a mile distant and make for the gaps in the line where the weak Guns are stood. A mistake made manifestly apparent as they fly into the plate glass window dangling some good distance up directly over the Magnet's head. Equally the reared bird is noted for its reliability and determination to do just exactly as it is told by its keeper and mentor and fly evenly and considerately over the centre of the line as per instructions and training. So why do they suddenly take collective leave of their better judgement and stream over the Magnet out at No. 1? To our disappointment and their lasting disadvantage?

Even shooting duck in the twilight there is no doubt as to which side of the pond the birds will flight to. In marked contradistinction to their habitual pattern over a succession of more or less successful flights when they have invariably gone to THIS side of the pond; now only THAT side of the water will do. Why? Because he's there. Obviously.

Is it mere luck? Does the bread always fall butter side down? Is the Pope really Catholic and what exactly is it that bears do in the woods? The only occasion when the Magnet's powers seem to wane are when you carefully rig the draw so as to get next to him and to share in some of this strange and irritating phenomenon. At which point it turns off like a tap and every bird in the district avoids him, or more particularly, you, as if you had "DANGER!!" tattooed on your forehead in letters of fire a yard tall.

Him they don't avoid at all, which is why when you return drive after drive empty handed, he is hefting a handful of pheasants into the game cart and saying "They all seemed to come across my left. Strange, because I'm not usually much good on that side."

Damn. Damn. Damn. Damn. Damn. Damn. And blast him.

SIBERIA

8

THE UNDER NINES

They are booted and spurred and anoraked and damp and hot and each clutching a pheasant as if their very lives depended on it and they are deeply, deeply happy and ever so slightly confused. They are booted and spurred and anoraked because that was the compromise agreed with their mother when they left this morning. "Yes, you can go beating, but you are to wear your anoraks and wellingtons and you will have your gloves on strings because that is where they will be most convenient and you will not lose them. Again. Yes, you can wear your Davy Crockett hat, if you absolutely insist. Spurs are for riding, darling, and today we are beating. All right, if you must, but if you lose them you won't have them for riding, will you? No, you can't wear a Barbour like Daddy; because you haven't got one. Well, you should have thought of that when you said you wanted the Thomas the Tank Engine one. Right, boots, hats, gloves, sticks. Set. Go. Have a lovely day. If you get too cold Daddy will bring you home."

Will he cocoa. Daddy is getting one of the few days a season Daddy gets these days, what with the ponies and the parties and the bouncy castles and school trips and visits to Granny and Grandpa at half term and all the other wretched paraphernalia which comes with parenthood. So for just as long as they are one nano-notch this side of hypothermic they are staying in the beating line and liking it.

And so they are delivered into the care and, as far as possible, the control, of the under-keeper on arrival and told to do as he says on pain of death. "Just you stay along o' me" says he "and keep them sticks tappin', and we'll all manage admirable." And

so as the horn goes for the first drive they dive straight in and attack the brambles like Conan on speed. And they hack and hew for all they are worth for, perhaps, five minutes. "Tom" they say, or as it might be Dick or Harry or Derek or Charlie, "we're stuck." And so Dick or Harry or Tom or Derek or Charlie duly detaches them from the bramble pile in which they are embedded and plonks them back on the ride along o' him where they mooch along desultorily sideswiping nettles until one of them pokes a bush and an old cock bursts out the other side with a squawk and a clatter leaving a small and startled bundle sitting on its bottom in the frost. "Pheasant ! Pheasant ! Pheasant ! Daaaaaaddy ! Gerrim! Gerrim! Daaaaaad! Pheaaaasant!" And as the birds begin to flush they are back and forth across the ride poking bushes here and there and exhorting Daddy with mounting frenzy to do one in on their behalf and to uphold the household honour.

And as they emerge finally from the wood, red-cheeked and glowing with exertion Daddy has duly executed a brace on their behalf with which they are issued for delivery to the game cart without delay and which they are therefore clutching with a sense of family pride and personal contribution that they have seldom before experienced. And why are they confused? Because on all sides in their tiny lives they are subtly advised that the whole experience is cruel and savage and gruesome and barbaric and fundamentally horrid and hideous and terribly, terribly wrong. And on the ground, or at least not very far from it, it turns out to be exciting, and thrilling and just so much fun.

OVER NINETY

He bin beatin' here and hereabouts man an' boy for t' thick end of a cent'ry and thur 'ent nartin' he hen't seen 'n hurd in thet time.

Of course, it was better when the old Major had the place. That was before the Great War. Oh, them were times. All the gentlemen and ladies would come down for the shooting parties and lunch was taken in a marquee set up for the week down by the lake. And didn't they shoot just? Two guns, sometimes three, and a cartridge boy for the loaders. Ooh, yus, we was cartridge boys now n' agin. An extra sixpence, that was. And then the Great War came and all the gentlemen were swept away in a much less agreeable shooting party in the mud of Flanders. And then Sir Charles had it, didn't he? And that took us up to the next round against the Hun. He was alright, was old Charlie, but he was never really the shooting man his father was, was he? And when we all, well, some of us any road, came back the second time, you could see his heart wasn't in the place. And then when his wife was took, well, he sort of lost interest. But what really done him was the horses. No. No. Not the betting. Not that he wasn't a gambling man for all that. Blas' there was some punting in them days. We heard 'em talk as we went round with the Guns, din't we? Hundreds on the turn of a card. Ho, yus. No, it was when the horses went from the land, and the tractors came. That'd be the sixties, I reckons. Forty or fifty great horses we had here. Shires and Suffolks. Gurt things they were. Old Jimmy, you remember Jimmy? Used to do a bit of keepering down the Long Wood, and a deal of poaching if'n I'm any judge.

Jimmy was the last of the lads here. Blas', but he loved them horses. Him 'n Charlie both. Broke both their hearts proper when the 'orses went. Young Charlie had it next an' he did keep a old Punch fur the game-cart like, an' fur occasions. But even that went when th' old boy finally got 'is ticket.

Now young Charlie, 'e is a shooting man. Don' reckon as how the big shoots will ever be back here whatever. Well, how would anyone afford it these days, for all Charlie's done alright, they do say, what with goin' t' the City an' all? No. No. Doesn't scarcely farm it a bit now. Well, just fur the look of it, really, an' fur the pheasants what with the covers an' the set-aside. Is'sa waste really, when you think.

Still, we puts on a few good pheasants for all that, and young Charlie's mates, well there's a few of them really can shoot, I tell yer. They claw them birds down every which way. Oh aye, one or two, they are something to see. Yew recall that American? French? Eytie, was he? Well, he was foreign, anyhow. But blas' could he shoot? Three dead in th' air. Single gun, an' all. I tell yew true. Three. Up an' under an'all. Three dead. Marvellous. Took me back, I can tell yew. I hen't seen the like since the old Count Pollywolly, Policey, old Charlie's mate - Polerenski – tha's the fellow. 'E was an Eytie. Russian, was 'e? 'E was a furreigner an all. I seen him do three. Tha' was with two guns mark yew. Was that the horn? Best we get started then.

UPWARDLY MOBILE

It might even be better, a little better, not much but some, if he didn't have such an irritating ring. A ring is a ring after all, but the Dambusters' bursting out of his pocket every five minutes just seems to make the whole thing infinitely worse.

There was a sharp intake of breath when first he arrived and clambered from his shiny Bavarian saloon while still concluding a conference call with Tokyo. "Hai! No. Sorry. Must go. I'm here. Sorry, there. No. Sayonara! Hi!" Even the other Guns are sucking their teeth and they are his mates. So far. Corporate jolly this may indeed be and as goodly a bunch of high net worth City wheeler dealers as you could shake a bonus cheque at, they may be, but they are civil enough for all that and take their shooting seriously and they are, if the truth be known, notoriously generous at the end of the day and so they are welcome, more or less, to have a crack at the pheasants from time to time.

But this is an asp even in their very bosom.

"Dah-dee-dah-dah-dah-da-da-da-dah!" "Hey! No, I'm shooting actually. Yeah! Right. Yeah! What? No, you're breaking up a bit. Dunno. Four hundred, I think. Yeah. Sure. Done. Cheers, mate."

Maybe if a spouse or partner were actually in labour, or a child or loved one were actually undergoing surgery during the course of the day, then it could be left on the game-cart? Maybe.

"Dah-dee-dah-dah-dah-da-da-da-dah!" "Hello. Oh, hi mate. No. First drive. Somewhere down the M4, mate. What? You're kidding right? No! Cool! See ya! Caio!"

Before drives. During drives. Between drives. Without concern. Without consideration. Apparently

without conscience. Would he treat dinner thus? He certainly does lunch.

"Dah-dee-dah-dah-dah-da-da-da-dah!" Clambering all over the furniture in pursuit of better reception with signally more enthusiasm than he showed for the morning's pheasants. "Hey! No. Lunch. Catch you later, mate." And guess whose battery charger fused the hotplate in the dining room and delivered cold custard with the cook's formerly renowned blackberry and apple crumble? No prizes.

The gun may be of indisputable quality. He may be suited and booted beyond criticism. He may even shoot the odd pheasant from time to time between calls. Then "Dah-dee-dah-dah-dah-da-da-da-dah!" "Yeah? No. Shooting, mate. Shooting. Bang! Bang! Yeah. Gotta go. Right and left coming up. Bye!" Keepers, beaters, hosts, cooks, pickers-up, guests, Guns and pheasants by now are all but queuing just to damn bust him in the mouth and hurl the tinkly trinket into the nearest pond.

In the end it is a fellow Gun who takes a hand. And for the last drive at least there is silence. By now however, the atmosphere is so polluted that the absence of the irritating little tinkle is quite as bad and it is almost a relief when it returns at tea. "Dah-dee-dah-dah-dah-da-da-da-dah!"

He's still talking as the keeper gives him a brace of birds. "Hang on a sec. Cheers, mate. Lovely. Nah. Keeper bloke. Yeah? Really? How much?……" and he's till talking as the glossy saloon wafts him down the gravel drive and away with a cheery toot of the horn. "Dah-dee-dah-dah-dah-da-da-da-dah!" Just when you think it can't get any worse.

THE PARTRIDGE PLONKER

It takes a certain sort of skill to be a good partridge Shot and a deal more besides to be a great one. And that is only to deal with the reared bird, let alone the wonder that is a covey of wild English partridges bursting over a hedge and flaring like a deranged Roman Candle gone berserk. Natural talent is a start. Added to which top notch hand eye co-ordination, above average speed, fitness, focus and concentration are all key and three weeks solid at the grouse before you start is a distinct advantage. Add to this volatile mix the necessary confidence to take birds just as they clear the hedge such that your shot whistles by only a few feet above the beaters' heads which is why the difference between a top partridge Shot and a plonker with an apparently total disregard for the welfare of the staff is finer than a lightweight Rizla. Except that the partridge professional has two birds down in front and another behind whereas the duffer has two beaters face down in the stubble in front and a picker up flat on his back behind. And that's quite a big difference. The fact is that he has been known to shoot pheasants quite well. Albeit quite modest pheasants. And he has shot ever so many clays down at the local shooting school which purport to imitate partridges and he powders pair after pair of those. It is just that they do just that. They imitate. They arrive in pairs. From a predictable direction and on a predictable trajectory and at a uniform speed. They do not come over the hedge in a tightly knit squadron of a dozen or so in a shifting pattern which explodes in all directions the minute you get your gun up. And they do not veer and jink such that the one you are just drawing a bead on suddenly looks out of range while the one that was tailender before now seems to be coming straight over your head in a way that makes it so reminiscent of the ones at the shooting school that you simply must check your swing and have a lash at him instead, or would do if the little bugger hadn't just vanished all of a sudden into thin air. Rather like your shot. Again. While the Gun next door has dropped another two in front and one behind. Again. All of which makes the whole thing incomparably worse. It is a rule as universal as it is absolute that in any line of Guns, but most particularly on a partridge day, a plonker will be between a couple of top killers. This is partly because two average Shots, to put it at its highest, together means a big hole in the line which the little partridges will seek out and exploit as an escape route without hesitation and so the captain will dispose his key killers through the line to maintain some semblance of competence; and partly because, if you are having a bit of an off day or are not really fit enough, or focused enough, or just plain good enough to be shooting really good partridges, on a bit of a breeze, really well then your neighbours will always seem to be in a wholly different league anyway and part of a carefully crafted plot to make you feel like a complete partridge plonker. Which is what you are and will remain until you focus, concentrate, stick with your bird, kill two in front and one more behind and move into the premier league. In other words, you plonker, relax.

BEATING BRIGADIER

"Just ease round a bit from the last peg and you should be able to cover the side of the wood too, in case any go back. If you're in any doubt, just ask the Brigadier. He'll be stopping on the hedge by the top end gate." And indeed he is. Not that he looks at first glance like a brigadier, but as you draw a little closer and note the pin holes in the shoulders of the worn leather jerkin over stiffly creased tweed, the 'kerchief squared off, and the short pipe jutting briskly between clenched teeth beneath the trim moustache you may recognize a certain strength of purpose about him. Standing erect by the fence tap-tap-tapping away with his blackthorn, while hooded eyes monitor the wind, the wood and the dispositions of Guns and beaters in the valley below. A polite "Good morning." And a tentative "D'you think I should stay just about here?" elicits a confirmatory drawl. "I should sconce yourself some little way to your left, if I were you. Just in that shadow by the mole hill. It'll be a trifle chillier out of the sun, but less windy and the birds won't pick you up as they round the corner till it's too late. If it's going to be too late for 'em, that is. You should have a shot or two anyway. " And there you have it really. Sit. Rep.:- Birds in wood. Met. Data:- Cold; some cloud cover; light breeze. Status:- Gun in position. Prognosis:- Likely to have some fun, if the shooter is up to snuff. Which remains to be seen. Report in full after drive. Over and out.

He used to shoot a good deal himself, of course, but age, what with the hip thing and the encroaching stiffness in his left arm, means that he is not as nimble as once he was and there aren't the invitations there used to be as the ranks of his friends have been progressively thinned. And he wouldn't buy a day either. Not quite the thing actually, for a start. The sort of thing a chap does, or doesn't. Probably couldn't afford it anyway these days, after the bloody pensions disaster. Cheats and swindlers the lot of them. Still, soldier on. At least the better half is in a better place, so she can't see what's left of the savings. Hey-Ho! Tap-tap. "Geddin, yer daft bird. Do as you're damn well told." But it's nice to get out of a frosty morning, and they are a jolly unit the beaters, and the Guns are by no means a bad crew either. The regulars that is. Not so sure about the let days, to be honest. Some are all right, but some of them are a complete shower. No other word for it. Shower. Most frightful oiks. And dangerous with it. Mark my words. Final straw, being shot by your own side. Shocking. Told 'em so too, and the boss. Don't think we shall be seeing them again. Good job. No, it's an agreeable day out, and a round or two of drinks afterwards with the men, that is, with the others. And at the end of the season we get a beaters day, which is thoroughly agreeable and the old bundook gets an outing. Rounds things off nicely, actually. I say, heads up. On your toes. Over. And again. Well done. I said we might get a bit of fun.

That "we", for those who care to notice it, is a compliment beyond treasure.

NEW GUN

He on time and he's smart and he's clean and he's terribly, terribly nice. As the result he sticks out like a sore thumb when the rest of the Guns turn up fifteen minutes later covered in yesterday's mud and nursing the most colossal hangovers from last evening's boisterous post shooting dinner and billiards fives session. He is fresh and pressed and clean and new. His boots are green and clean and his cartridge bag is brand spanking and polished like a favourite conker.

They are disreputable in tweed which is so elderly as to be threadbare where it is not patched after too many contretemps with barbed wire. Their boots are old and tackety and faded with use and their cartridges are stuffed carelessly into pockets from satchels that might have seen service in the Crimea. Their hats are almost beyond description. Battered and stained as if they have been dragged out from under the seat of the Land Rover where they were stuffed overnight to stop the damn dog chewing it to bits or reclaimed from the bottom of the game bag where something which has been festering for a while seems to have dribbled on it. His gun is a perfectly respectable and serviceable Spanish boxlock which he decided on after close and careful scrutiny of the books on the subject and long and earnest debate with his local gunshop and hangs from his shoulder in a stiff new waterproof sleeve.

They unship a wide and varied collection of elderly English sidelocks from boxes and cases heaped in the back of their wagons and shove them into stained sheepskin slips that seem to have been unearthed from the potting shed. And he is polite and deferential and eager to please and keen to fit in and determined to be, not just a good, but a sporting Shot. They are raucous and comfortable and shoot each other's birds knowing full well that there is no shot more sporting than to fold up your neighbour's right and left for him just as he's putting up his gun and then flatten his double miss

behind with a well directed choke barrel into the bargain. They insult one another interminably and roar with laughter whenever a pheasant hits the deck. They shoot like gods and drink like fish and their conversation is a continuous stream of shooting reminiscence, arcane references to obscure and antique jokes and heavily unsubtle commentaries on the downright reprehensible perversity of their complicated sexual preferences. Put short, he is the New Gun and they are the gnarled remnants of a crew that give a reasonable impression of having been shooting together since the Flood. And he is understandably nervous. As indeed are they. They introduce themselves by names which they none of them seem to use or to answer to. They greet their host with easy familiarity and astonishingly rude comments about the scarcity of his pheasants and they kiss his wife.

The New Gun is offered a wallet of peg numbers, but the captain has his thumb clamped firmly over all but one. This turns out to be between the captain and the oldest member where he is so manifestly on approval that a child could see it. They sing in the trailer as they are transported to the first drive. Who would not be nervous? We have all been here at one time or another. They have all been here at once time or another. They all joined this team as a New Gun once. And by the time he has shot a handful of decent birds and nailed one or two spectacular ones while double banking in the back row at the signature drive and got the nicknames sorted out and had a bit of a gargle at elevenses and picked up on some of the in-jokes and tried a few sallies of his own to general merriment and given as good as he got in the joshing between drives and over lunch and laughed and sung, and not shot low birds or the captain or the oldest member or the beaters, by the time he has done all of this, he is not yet perhaps an old hand but he is no longer the New Gun. Which is a huge relief to everybody. What a difference a day makes.

SMALL BORE

He shoots with guns of so exquisite a fineness that their barrels are handrolled on the thighs of Italian craftsmen of such unparalleled antiquity that they once made swords for Caesar's legions.

They are so light that he sometimes forgets whether he is holding them or not and stands, as the consequence, poised to address his grouse or perhaps partridge, maybe pheasant, with empty arms outstretched as if welcoming an old and sorely missed friend. His obvious refinement however is so extreme that the grouse, maybe pheasant, perhaps partridge, surrender to their inevitable doom and plummet notwithstanding to the ground behind his butt in a fit of terminal admiration of his ineffable good taste and heart-attack inducing style. He used to shoot with twelve bores like everybody else until his blossoming panache and burgeoning reputation drove him to lighter and faster twenties in pursuit of even greater speed and elegance. The twenties gave way to twenty-eights which were as slender as a pair of toothpicks and as deadly as the sting of the tiny funnel web spider. They lasted but a season until his new guns were ready. The new .410s are to the twenty-eights as gossamer is to a breezeblock. Their tempered aluminium actions and titanium breeches seamlessly blend the contemporary cutting edge technology of the space shuttle with traditional craftsmanship of Stradivarian heights while their engraving reflects both the artistry and refinement of the Renaissance.

Eschewing as he does more modern variations their finely figured stocks are of antique French walnut carved from the doors of an armoire that once graced the palace of Cardinal Richlieu himself and the matching rods are tipped with gilded tools from Asprey. Their lizard skin cases are lined with the same velvet from which the slippers of Marie Antoinette's ladies of the bedchamber were constructed in order that they did not inadvertently awaken their sovereign queen as they crept hither and yon drawing curtains and warming the crinolines. The guns are, in short, a bit like their owner being small but, in his own opinion, perfectly formed and fantastically good looking and terribly, terribly good at their job. Which is, of course, to shoot grouse or, as it might be, partridges, or indeed and for that matter, pheasants. Not that his job is to shoot although he seems to spend enough time doing it that he could make a career out of it if he had a mind to. His job, whatever that is, is simply a means to an end. The end being for him to shoot so absurdly well that he could use an air pistol, nay a catapult and dried peas and still kill more pheasants or, as it might be, partridges or for that matter grouse than anyone else in the line and do it altogether more elegantly and gracefully and generally shinily at the same time.

With his platinum coated, gold inlaid and pinpoint perfect rose and scroll engraved air pistol with walrus ivory grips and black pearl foresight bead. Or indeed the lightweight Kevlar graphite frame catapult with the hand-spun ultra-fine rubber culled drop by drop from ancient Burmese rubber trees that has been chewed by virgin silk worms for a year before being plaited strand by individual strand in the organically warmed and humidity controlled air of an Icelandic natural hot spring sauna by Inuit elders in order better to accommodate the perfectly shaped peas handpicked from selected plants on the southern slopes of a foothill in the Himalayas and….. Oh, don't be so ridiculous. Get a life!

BIG BORE

"Of course, I used to shoot with standard loads. I think that we all do, in the beginning. But then some of us move on, don't we, you know? Onward and upward. I mean the one ounce round is alright for the journeyman shooter; but as one gets more experienced, you know, I found that they were not really connecting at the sort of birds that one is presented with on really top class shoots. You need something faster and heavier, you know?" What he's looking for, you know, is a fat lip the way he keeps droning on and on and on about his bloody bullets. "It took me ages, of course, to find just the right combination. I tried competition loads. They were fast, but they simply weren't heavy enough for the sort of shooting I do now, you know? And I tested bigger shot sizes, right down to 3s and 4s but they didn't pattern well enough at long range, you know?" Of course we know. We know because he never stops telling us about his double gun days in the West Country and his 400 plus bags in Yorkshire where the cartridge to kill ratios are no better than 12:1 even for a top team like he shoots with let alone a bunch of mere mortals like the rest of us who would be lucky to break 20:1 with our sad little shells. "In the end I simply had to go direct to the manufacturers and explain to them what was wanted. They took my point in the end." And his money, no doubt, cartridge manufacturers not being quite as slow off the mark as he seems to think. "So now I have 'em specially loaded. I suspect they are selling them on as their new Supa Hi Powa High Pheasant Ultra, but mine have a bit extra in them even than those. They're faster than an F-16 on departure and heavier than a freight train on arrival." As it would appear when we watch him putting his 2¾", high brass 1½oz nickel cadmium coated, depleted plutonium total psycho headbanger cartridges through his lightweight game guns. "On my third set of barrels, you know!" he yells through the din as they go off with a roar like an artillery shell and a kick like an Arkansas mule on diabolic steroids which leaves him with a slightly faraway look and somewhat slurred conversation by midmorning. "The p-point iss thad I gan shude almozed ever day widdem an doan ged t-tied or nuffing." as he explains over drinks while broadcasting sloe gin down his waistcoat from a shaking hand. "An I shude a g-gud deal, y'know."

As he demonstrates by taking birds well over his neighbours' neighbours. Just because he can. Which isn't really a very sporting thing to do. Which is actually the point he misses with the same depressing regularity as he hits unfeasible birds with his preposterously powerful bullets. As he stresses rather more loudly than necessary, deafened as he is by the concussion as much as the noise, at lunchtime. "FAC TIS…ER..FAC TIS….MMMMM…S-S-SHOODING WID O-O-ONNERY CARRIGES M-M-MEENS SHUDING ONNERY BUDS. I-I-IZ TOO….TOO..TOO EEZA; WON MY VOOO! UZ…UZ..UZ WHY I DOAN D-D-DO ID EN M-M-M-ORE." he bawls across the table with his eyes rolling in opposite directions as he spoons another helping of steak and kidney into his lap, pours gravy over his crumble and downs another glass of claret over his shoulder to wash down the Anadin he just put up his nose for the headache. "E-E-EVERBOY SHOOD DRY U-U-UT. S-S-SOON SORDA MEN FROM…FROM…FROM…. OH BUGRIT I GARN MEMMER WOD! FINK NEEDA LIDDLE L-L-L-LIDOWN FWILE."

Oh dear! Poor old big bore. It seems to make him happy though and that's the main thing. It is supposed to be fun, after all, you know. When he comes round you might remind him, why don't you?

THE OLDEST GUN

He mistook the Ark for a game-cart and lobbed in his brace of birds with a brisk word of congratulation to Noah about the straightness of his beating line. He has fought in more wars than you could shake a stick at, and has won most of the important ones more or less single handed. He tends towards the view that young people would be well advised to spend a little time between school and university finding themselves a decent war to get mixed up in, since it gives a sense of perspective later in life. A combination of the dicky hip, sundry wounds, chronic but intermittent gout and a lifelong addiction to rough cut shag means that he is incapable of moving to any outlying peg and the role of walking Gun is a mystery to him. He puts 5,000 rounds a season through his old Holland, which his Grandfather, secure in the knowledge that the thing was within a micron of being out of proof then and was a liability to anyone within thirty yards, presented him as a gift on his 21st birthday, and which has not been within a mile of a smith's since.

No one can remember when he joined the team, or whether he ever did. When they turned up to shoot, there he was - and he has been coming ever since. There may very well be another shoot on the estate next door who are still waiting for him and wondering if it was something they said.

He shoots from a stick and he seldom misses. Not that he lets off terribly often. Many years of patience spent behind a rock or in a trench or up a tree waiting for some variety of foreigner to stick his head into view has given him a very clear picture of the right moment to participate. Accordingly he demolishes a limited number of selected birds - presumably those with a goodly quantity of white to their eye - and ignores the rest, be they high, wide or handsome. Since he is - selectively - as deaf as a post to boot, yelling at him that there are birds roaring past, over or by him will do no good flat. He has been shooting here since before you were born and knows every drive like the back of his hand. Backwards, forwards and sideways. When the keeper attempts a brave new departure by reversing one of the main drives, he will snort derisively, announce loudly that every pheasant in the place will leg it up the side hedge if you try it that way, and spend the whole of the next drive fiddling with his pipe. The fact that he has been shooting here since before you were born and has seen all the drives under every circumstance and that he is almost certainly right only serves to make this habit more annoying.

Equally he has a habit of cornering the younger Guns after shooting and embarking upon his life story. Unfortunately he always chooses the one day when you absolutely, positively must get away upon pain of death and so you cut him short to your embarrassment and his chagrin. Which is a pity, because you don't get the chance every day of the week to meet the man who slept with Mata Hari, rode with Lawrence, blew up Rommel's fuel dumps, did time garrotting bad hats in the Balkans, hunted with Hemingway, double dated with Erroll Flynn, invented the telescopic sight and designed a salmon fly so lethal that it was banned by Act of Parliament.

THE LAIRD

There he stands on the drawbridge. Or as it might be in the Long Gallery. Or on the gravel sweep before the battle-mented turrets or behind the third butt in the line. Whatever. Wherever. Kilted and bonneted in the clan tartan. Leaning on his ramshorn crook. Eyes drifting towards the far hills across the loch where the ravens circle lazily in the thermals and the stags roar in the corries and the grouse call in the heather "Go back! Go back! Go back! RRRRrrrrrrrrr!" Waiting for the tourists. Be they gun toting Americans or camera clicking Japanese. Be they trophy hunters from Europe or grouse shooters from the City or salmon fishermen from far, far away. It makes not a scrap of difference. As long as they pay. And he will keep his counsel and his countenance.

Time was when you if owned everything you could see from those self-same battlements, that was enough. Those were the days when a stag from the hill or a grouse from the moor or a salmon from the river was a laird's pleasure as well as his right and proper recreation. But what with three generations of devil may care management, the death duties and the Lloyds debacle, these days the laird can scarcely afford to keep the rain out of the place, let alone heat the more habitable parts and the idea of having a day at the grouse just for fun is about as sensible as the estimate for shoring up what remains of the west wing. Now he is no more or less of a fixture and fitting in his own home than the suits of

armour that stand rustily to attention in the hall or the great stags who stare down glassily from the shadowy heights of the billiards room. He meets, he greets. He is affable and agreeable. In short he is, to his lasting chagrin, affordable.

It was, of course, ever thus. The difference was that then the laird himself could afford it. And gradually, gradually as the family fortune dwindled and the debts mounted the plain and peeling truth became increasingly apparent. The sheep kept the shepherd, the grouse their keeper; the salmon just about kept the gillie and the stags supported the stalker. But who would keep the laird and the roof over his head? It was either go to work or go away and with a heritage that stretches back to the Bruce and beyond being the last of the long line of lairds was not an option. And so it was work.

And now he stands on the drawbridge, or the battlements or the ballroom or wherever and waits for the tourists to arrive in order that he can meet and greet and be affable and agreeable and informative. And he will earn his living like everyone and everything else on the great estate and he will keep his counsel and his countenance; for though the house and the grounds and the sport may all be available for rent to all and sundry, the day that the laird's pride is for sale, that is a day you'll never see.

THE GROUSE KEEPER

The grouse keeper is not, as anyone will tell you, like other men. For openers he spends his working life on the high moors where the sun beats down relentlessly during the brief summer months, and where the wind and worse howl for the rest of the year. Accordingly the grouse keeper looks like a rock that has been left out in the weather. Worn smooth in parts, but with cracks here and there you could plant spuds in. And he has a sailor's eyes. Hooded against the weather and forever focused on the distant horizons. The grouse keeper spends most of his time alone and therefore develops a fierce independence which can make him intolerant of the low ground folk; he's probably too polite to say so except under extreme circumstances, but he knows that the rest of us are just jessies, to be honest.

Consider this; when the Guns have departed, and the shooting parties have packed up for the season the grouse keeper walks his moor counting the stock remaining. After anything but a grim year the chances are that there will be too many grouse left. And too many grouse means a higher chance of disease come the spring and less birds for the owner next season. So throughout the back-end days of the season, yea, even up to the 10th December, he will harry and pursue the wee birds in the company of his dogs to disperse and thin them. He will, of course, concentrate on the old birds. How he can tell an old bird from a young bird once the coveys become packs, or even among the singletons he encounters, is a mystery vouchsafed only to grouse-keepers. You and I might be able to spot a squeaker in August, once we have it in hand, but the grouse keeper can pick the old cocks out in a crowd and nails them ferociously at maximum range and from all points of the compass. Which done he retires to his cottage for the rest of the winter.

As the blizzards finally clear he is walking the moor again looking for paired birds and contemplating his burning programme. A peat fire is a terrible thing, which can burn for days and loiter for weeks under ground smouldering away like a genie in a lamp. We live in terror of fire. The grouse keeper, though, regularly torches his domain in controlled burns to encourage the young heather. Then he protects the nesting birds day and night from crows and foxes, stoats and rats, trapping and despatching 24 hours a day for those vital and dangerous weeks, as the hens sits tight on their clutches. Once the chicks are hatched he spends his nights on all fours in said heather catching the wildest game birds in these isles in a landing net in order to vaccinate them against their mortal enemy - the worm. The worm is the only creature on God's own earth that frightens grouse keepers. You can take your Beast of This or your Devil O'That, your roaring lion going about seeking whom he may devour, and bottle them frankly, but mention the worm and he pales and jabbers.

Then having counted his birds, shot them and harried them, watched and counted them again, burned his ground, nursed, dosed and protected his birds from every sort of peril, and all of this on his tod for the most part, mark you, he spends the summer shoving them over the butts for the rest of us to shoot. Shoot at anyway. Go figure. Not, definitely not, as other men.

THE EURO SHOT

Like an October pheasant floundering over the wire of the release pen, the Euroshot is a target unworthy of a true sportsman. So here goes. Shaving-gear in the hatband, obsessed with the size of his trophy and a predilection for arriving in the field in only what can be described as suede hot pants. And that's only the northerners. Moving steadily south or downhill as it is sometimes described, and we encounter aftershave, smarm and garlic, all in industrial quantities. They mangle the language, seduce the staff and execute the livestock. And then they buy our gunmakers. The bounders have zips in their wellingtons, for heaven's sake. And look confused when you explain who invented them.

Mark you, they are nothing compared to your actual Mediterraneans. Over and unders, shoot at anything that moves – and most things that don't. Drink like fish – from the bottle – sleep all afternoon and can't be trusted with donkeys. They pee in the garden, flounce about draped in lambswool pullies, have gold teeth, no morals and tend to disappear when the bill arrives. They are low, sleek, garish, fast, thirsty and unreliable; just like their lousy sports cars. And to crown it all they have this universal tendency at the end of the day, when the meagre bag is laid out on the lawn – two starlings, a Blackfaced Hardwicke, three pheasants, eight rabbits and the under-gardener – of setting fire to the hedge and playing a trumpet voluntary in honour of the dear departed. Well, really. It's just too easy and we should not go down that road, however much fun it is.

The Germans contribute significantly to the maintenance of the place in Scotland, while the Belgians and the Dutch consistently prop up the prices of agricultural land in East Anglia, which they largely built – or salvaged – in any event. The French bring their own claret and a stream of unfeasibly pretty girlfriends; while the Spanish have provided everybody for a generation with his first 20-bore. And the Italians, if we are good, will let us have a go in the two-seater as well as making the only over and unders which don't look like agricultural machinery. And while we are on the candour jag, we ourselves are a bunch of bulky, red-faced individuals who tend to have a good deal of breakfast, and dinner, for that matter, smeared across our waistcoats. We wear inherited trousers the size of zeppelins, live in abject poverty in freezing-cold houses where we engage in unnatural practices learned when our mad parents abandoned us, aged nine, on the steps of some Gothic workhouse. And whenever someone is named Tom or Dick or Harry, we insist, for no particular reason that anyone can remember, on calling them Stinks. Bunny and Pongo.

We are all Europeans now, I'm told. So there.

THE AMERICAN

He started out as a grease monkey on the line down on the shop floor but he was foreman a decade gone and by the time another decade had passed he was running the shop. Then he leveraged everything they had and bought the damn company. He had a lucky break when he saw the gap in the market and geared up big time when everyone else was scaling back and, boy, did they ever clean up. Then it was just a question of waiting till the big boys saw the light and bought him out. He stayed on the first time as a sort of president, for the look of the thing, but when they spun the whole damn division out he cashed in a pile of options and just bailed out to go hunting. And Mary Beth has been there right alongside the whole durned ride. "I said to that li'l' lady, I said, when we was first steppin' out, I said "You stick with me, kid, an' yew'll never want for nuthin'!" an' was I right. Li'l' darlin', was I right?" And Mary Beth looks up from knitting bootees for the grandkids, notwithstanding that she could buy Bootees 'r Us happen she felt the need, and smiles "Damn right, you were right, Big Man, damn right. You never broke a promise, your whole life long, Sweetpea!" And now they travel the world absorbing culture and thinning the wildlife as they go. Safaris in Africa, fishing in Tierra del Fuego, a glimpse of the Eiffel Tower as they swing through Paris for some shopping and fancy food and annually to Scotland for the grouse.

"Grouse is the finest hunt in the world." he declares positively. "Damned if I ken see why you people let those wise-ass politicians, north an' south, try so damned hard to f…., save your presence there, sweetheart, …fix to screw it up for you so completely. It's a goddamn…. sorry, EmBee …

national asset, like the queen. They should be preservin' an' promotin' 'em both 'stead of doin' 'em down as they do! An' I'm a republican! No better 'n communists, my view!" In support of which view he and Mary Beth fly in once a season in the Gulfstream for a fortnight on the moors. Each year involves a trip through the West End in advance of the journey north to collect new matching suits and boots and usually to pick up a slack handful of game guns from one or other noted emporium. The latest, a trio, have taken umpteen years to build or more particularly to engrave with pictures of the house back home on the action of the No.1, "Home is the most important thing in a man's life, an' a princess to run it."; the corporate head-office on the No.2 – "Never forget what makes all the shoppin' possible, says I, an' I should know!" - and portraits of the grandkids on the No.3, "They are the future, after all." These are not for using, you understand; these will go into the vault at home, along with the dozens of other pairs and rarities, for the look of the thing. "Just perfection, ain't they?" What he uses, and uses to great effect it must be said, and so he should given the work he inflicts on them every year both here and at pheasants in Yorkshire and doves in Cordoba and guineas in Africa and duck on the Mekong delta as well as at home, is a modest pair of Brownings. "Best damn guns in the world. Designed by an American, made in America, used by Americans. All over the globe. Mayn't be pretty but they sure ain't afeared of hard work, they pays their way an' they won't let you down." Much like their owner then.

THE WILDFOWLER

Instantly recognisable by the fact that he is utterly unrecognisable. From the balaclava helmet underneath the Russian fur hat at one end, through the pneumatic vastness of well padded waterproofs in the middle to the colossal waders at the bottom end, the wildfowler is uniformly clad in mud. Not merely mud coloured but actual mud. And not just any old mud, such as you might pick up in a field in which through oversight you skidded or indeed a ditch into which one might inopportunely plummet; but mud such as is found only in the most remote regions of these isles and then a little way beyond that.

For the wildfowler's domain lies below the high water mark, and whether it be coast, estuary, river or mere it is out on the flats, beyond the creeks or below the banks that the best mud can be found, for here be fowl. And not just any old fowl either. You or I might account for the occasional mallard during a shooting day, or even a teal, but the wildfowler is after wilder game. Wigeon, Mallard, Pochard and Gadwall. Goldeneye and Scoter (Velvet as well as Common), Scaup, Pintail and Shoveller. Plover, Godwit and Redshank. And the geese of course, Whitefront, Pinkfoot, Greylag, and Bluish under the Armpit. No, you're right, that one was made up. Nonetheless the wildfowler is able to distinguish between each of these and confidently raises his gun to each and all - in the dark. For the final feature of wildfowling is that it must be undertaken largely in the middle of the night. And with the biggest guns that may conveniently be lugged the great distances involved and let off without sustaining serious, too serious, injury.

Thus when the rest of us are returning from a day in the field, the wildfowler is packing for the journey. All through the night he drives to some far flung and remote spot unpolluted by mortal men - other than wildfowlers. Here he envelops himself in many layers of vests and woolly underthings, covered in many more layers of shirtings and woolly overthings, topped off with an impermeable layer of rubber and muddy outerthings. Then he grasps his great double 8 bore to his bosom and strides off into the dark to find some decent mud. Once having discovered, by virtue of falling into several, a likely looking - or more probably feeling - salting, creek or dyke, the wildfowler embeds himself in its comfortable mud and waits for dawn or the tide; whichever arrives first.

If it is the dawn he waits some more until the fowl begin to move. This they do in wide circles around those ditches and creeks which are inhabited by fowlers. After an hour or so the fowler becomes sufficiently frustrated that he lets off his great gun anyway and begins to stumble home. At which point the tide arrives. Cut off from any effective route back to civilisation by the rising waters, the wildfowler spends the next four hours until the tide begins to ebb perched atop a muddy island taking comfort from the bleakness of his surroundings and solace from the howling of the wind. If the tide rises further, the fowler sits tight, dismantles his gun and uses the barrels as a snorkel until the water goes down. For this reason 8 bores always have three foot barrels giving rise to the expression "going the last yard."

Wildfowlers disdain other shooters because of the vastness of their bags, and venerate Sir Peter Hawker because he was the last wildfowler who actually shot something.

THE PIGEON SHOOTER

Swathed from head to foot in the last word Cammo, it is sometimes hard to tell the pigeon shooter from the tree. Out on the stubbles, however, he stands out like the proverbial rugby ball on a billiards table. And there is the noise, of course, since his every movement is accompanied by the sound of a mighty rushing wind as various layers of man-made fibre abrade one another and create a lightening storm of static.

Crouched in a ditch or under a hedge or lurking at the foot of a long wood, the pigeon shooter diligently sets out his stall. Decoys are dangled in the trees above, planted out on the crop, in front and set about, head to wind obviously, to attract the passing traffic. Feeders, wobblers and bobbers are variously pegged, pinned and inflated and merry-go-rounds, gliders and flappers are set up and powered by strings attached to the shooter's outlying limbs, or by cables attached to car batteries and small portable generators.

The hide is then constructed by hammering a series of modest girders into the ground at intervals, from which is suspended several more yards of camouflage netting and against which are set a selection of branches, twigs, leaves, fertiliser bags, tractor tyres and sundry parts of a Cortina in order to recreate the proper look of an average hedge. Inside, the pigeon shooter ensconces himself on a collapsible chair with his binoculars, a short-wave radio for communication with base, a portable radar screen and a sack of cartridges close to hand, and avails himself on the large flask or canteen which will sustain him through the afternoon.

The pigeons, meanwhile, are gathered for a meeting round the gas gun on the far side of the Old Sixty Acre. From time to time one of them will clap by the pigeon shooter just to see if he is ready yet to be persuaded to lug his gear to the other end of the field. Or whether he still harbours hopes of a record bag. When these occasional observers find themselves sidestepping the odd desperate shot at eighty yards out and more they know that they have another Cammo scalp for their sitty tree.

MRS JUDGE

It's not her real name, of course, any more than Digger's or Stumpy's or Chip's. Digger drives the digger, see; and Stumpy has only to grin at you to see where his name comes from and Chip's old man was Arthur Block, known as Chopper for obvious reasons. Mrs Judge first came to the shoot with her husband who was a circuit judge, for real, known to all and sundry as Just Judge, or JJ, which he was, after all; and it was the keeper, inevitably, whose memory is shaky but whose word is law who applied the soubriquet to Mrs Judge when he was trying to attract her attention betimes. In those days she was what we call a peg wife; small and pretty though there was something about the steady gaze and amused detachment which argued steel not far beneath the surface of Mrs Judge. She's what they call hereabouts "A right determined lady." And with the passage of time the dog made three. That dog had a litter and it was all downhill from there really, but things really took off when JJ died while still only in his middle years. "Sent down for good!" said Mrs Judge, at the service, "And he hadn't done half his sentence." And then she wiped her eye, blew her nose and focussed on her dogs. There was steel indeed, not far below the surface of Mrs Judge. And as it turned out she had a real way with dogs. She started with pretty little cockers and when all is said and done, it is the cockers which still give her the real pleasure, though she has teams of Labradors in all three colours so "I can tell what day of the week it is!" as she puts it. Which is as well because she picks up three days a week minimum on shoots around the county and indeed round the country, pretty much solidly from August to February. That's how good they are, you see, Mrs Judge's dogs. There are those who will tell

you that they are the children she and JJ never had, but you would have to say that the children got off pretty lightly because Mrs Judge trains her dogs hard and works them just as hard. No soppy sofas, chewy treats and warm hearthrugs for Mrs Judge's dogs. They live in kennels and get a cupful of high concentrate dry mix twice daily and are worked from dawn till dusk year round. And if one of them, any of them – for there are no favourites – should step out of line, then Mrs Judge is a sight to see. And to hear, for that matter.

And as it turned out Mrs Judge was a perfectly apt title that the keeper bestowed on her all those seasons past because she does a deal of judging too now one way and the other. She is highly regarded in the field trial world, of course, her own dogs, when she enters them these days, rarely being out of contention, but more now as a judge around the region. She'll don a bowler at the hound show too because her encyclopaedic knowledge of dogs extends beyond her own preferred breeds and her eye for a good 'un is uncanny. She's not slow to spot a bad 'un either and has little brief for social reports and psychology from her seat on the bench as a lay magistrate, and while her powers there are limited it is perhaps just as well because Mrs Judge has little truck with repeat offenders in her kennels or in her court or in her life. And woe betide therefore the persistent petty felon or indeed and for that matter the visiting Gun who fails to notify her properly of a pricked bird or who can't mark a fall with pin-point accuracy. She may still be small and pretty underneath her Barbour and overtrousers and boots and may yet twinkle with the best but be under no illusions there is steel not very far beneath the surface of Mrs Judge.

THE LOADER

There is a story of a Gun who went to a big day at the grouse and who was introduced to his loader who turned out to be a sleepy eyed exquisite who was staying in the big house and had volunteered for the exercise. As the first covey scorched the heather of the butt the Gun issued his two shots and felt for his second gun; to find nothing. Somewhat miffed he asked how he had done. "I don't know about you, " came the drawled response, "but I got one and missed one."

A good loader, and the loader just described was not a good loader, is a combination of many things. He is, all at once, servant, coach, spare eyes and ears, confidence booster, consolation provider, helpmeet, shield on shoulder, confidant and, with luck, friend. And all of this on short acquaintance. There was a time when loaders were just that. Chaps had loaders and that was what loaders did; and over time the relationship bloomed and blossomed until the chap and his loader functioned as one. Very few Guns today are fortunate enough to have such an assistant. Even fairly recently it was more likely than not that an occasional loader would be the keeper from a neighbouring shoot, released from other duties for the day. Now, however, when confronted by an occasional loader the visiting Gun is likely to find a fellow Gun who is loading because it is the next best thing to him shooting. And he may be a shepherd or a tractor driver or he may be a neurosurgeon or the Chief Constable for the area. There simply is no knowing. But if he is smart and efficient, with a neat suit and clean boots and if he handles your guns with a proper care and appreciation and doesn't burst out laughing because they are not consecutive serial numbers and are, indeed, by different – though respectable – makers; and if he is there with the spare as you drop your second bird in front and says "Well done. Coming half left!" as he thrusts it into your palm, as perhaps the theatre sister might slap a retractor into his own under different circumstances, and keeps low as he swivels to eject the spent shells and is back with "One down. Coming dead ahead!" as you change again; and if at the whistle he gives you a glimpse of the empty chambers as he slips one gun away and says something along the lines of "Eight in front and six behind, by my reckoning. Well done, I think we've held our own." then the chances are you will have a thoroughly enjoyable day and a new friend by the end of it.

Although you will very possibly never be entirely free of the suspicion, probably justified, that had the positions been reversed he might have done rather better.

LE GRAND FROMAGE PLUS FORT

There's them as dips a toe; there's them as takes a dive; and there's them as does a depth-charge off the toppest of top boards. Likewise there are those who shoot, some who shoot a lot and those who just embrace the whole thing in a complete bearhug and squeeze it until it's eyes water and it's mouth works guppy-like for breath.

The Range Rover Vogue Luxe (Special Edition) is a given, the personalised number plate "H181RDS" might be forgiven, and the headrests within containing DVD screens the better to review and consider his performance, recorded drive by drive and shot by shot by a retained camera-man, during the wearisome journey home, just might be for entertaining the children; but the ensemble which emerges goes beyond these trivial indulgences.

There's tweed; there's loud tweed, there's bungalow checks; and then there is the clan tartan made up into a suit of dazzling hue and abundant capacity, with a matching deerstalker hat, and a full length cape billowing beyond. And field boots buffed, by his batman no doubt, to Brigade of Guards glossiness peeking through thoroughly blancoed spats whereon twinkle tiny brass crest encrusted buttons.

And while we are on the subject of boots, who has not encountered the natty fitted mahogany gun-safe cum drinks cabinet and dog basket in the back of a Range Rover? Hah! Now let your mind wander towards an antique brass and crocodile-hide cabin trunk, early Vuitton, converted to contain the annual output a small private distillery, or chateau perhaps, even both, with guess whose name on the labels, and crystal of course. With a matching three tier gun-case and humidor which holds an abundance of Cuban torpedos above with a garniture of London's finest nestling below. And don't forget the cartridge magazine, and bags, which complete the set.

The brace of silver grey Weimeranas lounge on a cushioned platform, in matching plaid, which folds to nothing at elevenses time, above this plethora of former reptiles. There are antique ivory pins to allocate the pegs, Georgian silver clickers to count the shots and a drop-dead gorgeous girlfriend, in matching gear, to mark the fallen. There are no runners because despite shooting only the highest and fastest, he seldom misses. And nor he should; he shoots more days in the season than you get shots off in a day, and his global season is longer than a teenager's sigh. The outlay is as breathtaking as the suit.

The extravagance is famous. In addition to which his largesse is generous, his generosity notorious and his jokes more salacious than a five bob hooker. And he keeps inviting you back, which is all to the good, because otherwise you'd just have to hate him to death, which would scarcely be the act of a fellow sportsman.

And you thought you were taking things seriously?

THE POACHER

The fact that he is inclined to "tek a auld heer noon agin" is bucking for worst kept secret in the neighbourhood. The best kept is the fact that he does most of his shopping at the supermarket, but you can't mump too many pints from visitors with wild tales of the nine items or less check-out, now can you? And there was a time, to be sure, when he would sidle up the spinney after a cock bird or lay a wire under a gate for old puss. And he knows the hows of it. How to take a pheasant with raisins and a horsehair, or how to squeak in a fox, and he knows these woods as well as any man. By day or night. And the keeper knows he knows. Which is one reason he comes beating every shoot day. Better to have the poacher inside the tent and going home with a tenner and a brace than working the outside with a grudge and a muffled .410. Not that he used to use it very often. He can heft a bird from its roost as you or I would lift a book from the shelf, and think less of it by the way.

Much has changed now of course. The woods are full of strangers. In daylight the ramblers in their fluorescent anoraks, loud and lost; the mountain bikers - all sweat and lycra; and at night the dangerous angry men who come with a van after the poults in the pens. They go about their business with lamps and curses and care little how much noise they make. A stave or a boot or a sawed-off even will substitute for silence and finesse as occasion serves. Not for them the moonlit stroll, the stalk and the snatch.

After a shoot day he may very well take a circuit of the woods. You can always pick up a few pricked birds that have been overlooked or which have perched and fallen since the Guns and dogs moved on. If he should bump into the keeper he will hand over the birds to be added to the bag for the day, though like as not the keeper will tell him to keep them. There's little enough value in a bird in the hand these days. His old lurcher will amble along at his heels. She used to be a great one for "the rarebits end t'haars" but she is feeling her years now and while the spirit is as willing as ever, the flesh tends to lose it on the turns and anyway her eyes are none too good into the bargain.

All of which the keeper knows perfectly well; but poachers are like foxes. You can never be completely rid of them and nor should you be. Better to have one you know and recognise on the ground, than any number of occasionals or migrants. Then you know where you are. Or at least where he is. At least on shoot days.

GRUMPY OLD BART

The bathwater ran cold. Breakfast was late, and chilly as a witch's when it did finally turn up. Without the paper, would you believe? Don't even begin to commiserate about the traffic. I mean to say, where are all these people going at this time of the morning? They should start earlier, or work nearer to home, or somewhere else. And the map was no bloody good either. Can't think whose idea that was. There should be signs. Someone should put a few up. Well, someone should be made to put a few up. Several. Lots, in fact. He has to, after all. Damn National Trust have killed almost every tree in the park, nailing signs here, there and everywhere, so the punters can find the Tea Rooms without getting lost in the gloomy interior of the front drive. Whereas he needs planning permission for a post and rail fence just to keep them off the croquet lawn. Unbelievable.

He only got the invitation at the last minute, couple of months ago, so he must be a second stringer anyway. And then the gun was at the menders because he hadn't got round to collecting it. And when he got there he was advised that he should have a thou' of these newfangled cartridges to be going on with, and the cost of those nearly delivered a seizure. Just who exactly is going to arrest him if he should pot a mallard off his own pond with a perfectly ordinary cartridge? They should try. He's been on the Bench for thirty years or more. Goes with the territory really; and he's damned if he's going to be hauled up for a spanking in front of himself for letting off lead instead of some fancy new concoction that can't be pronounced without firing your dentures across the dinner table. Dammit.

So what are we milling about here for then? If people can't turn up on time they should be left behind. He's made it, after all, notwithstanding the horrors which are inevitably encountered the moment you set foot out of doors these days. Why can't others have the same common courtesy? Politeness of princes, that is. Not that there is much to rush for. The keeper has probably only just started blanking in the first drive. Bugger was probably still laid in bed not half an hour ago. Time was he'd have been up at first light, before, dogging in and checking on the whereabouts. Then we might have stood a chance of starting on time. As it is we will have to wait forty minutes on our pegs before a bird of some description puts in a belated appearance. Looks like rain too. Forty minutes in the freezing drizzle, just because you can't get the staff these days. Whatever happened to the work ethic?

And when the birds do pitch up, they won't be much to write home about. If he's told them once here, he's mentioned it a dozen times, they should put sewelling across the drive at the start of the plantation, then the birds won't bunch so. Like banging your head against a brick wall. They're all the same these days; three months course and they know it all. Mark you, the numbering has been fixed so there is little point in taking a lot of cartridges anyway. Plain as the nose on your dial. Assuming that is that the drives are in the usual order. Look, the middle Guns all have notable pheasant shoots which have yet to get into their main coverts, while the peripherals are the partridge men whose invitations have been enjoyed already. Cynical, moi? I should cocoa. Common sense.

I suppose they'll all want driving about all day too? Why can't people get their own, There'll be mud everywhere and the old trout will go ballistic when she sees the damage. Come on then, we might as well make a start. For what it's worth.

THE BLOATED PLUTOCRAT

He arrives, not in one Range Rover, but two. Or more particularly, he and his loader arrive in one, while his dogs and their handler turn up in the other. On his peg, on his shooting stick, the extra-broad hand-stitched pigskin seat squeaks comfortably against the soft, hand-woven, estate tweed-cashmere-mix-covered plutocratic bottom. The immediate vicinity is wreathed in fragrant smoke that dribbles from the Cuban El Colossale No. 1 Super Uniquo that is clamped between perfect teeth that are both testament and advertising for the cutting edge of modern orthodontics.

As the first carefully composed flock of birds are massaged off the runway by the keepers, his loader leans forward and murmurs a soft alert into the electronically sealed world of the Bloated Plutocrat. The European edition of the Journal is briskly folded and cast to the manicured sward beneath soft Schneider field-boots and the phone is disconnected. One dolphin-leather-gloved hand snaps back for the birds-eye maple grip of the Purdey proffered by his man. Squinting through the pink lenses of the Pengtsdorff und Schiller shades he shoots once, twice, into the deepest part of the cloud. Birds tumble nearby as he reaches for his second gun and adds another brace to his mounting score. The loader dutifully clicks twice to record the event for the gold-tooled Game Book. It is illustrated with original oils by very famous artists, featuring the Bloated Plutocrat in a variety of exotic locations in the world's great helicopter-accessible wildernesses, with his foot on the necks of a panoply of recently deceased wildlife.

Properly satisfied with the results of his efforts, the Bloated Plutocrat subsides once more to mop his excited brow with a scented square and to take a pull of the Trafalgar brandy from his heavy silver flask. Then he centres once more the smouldering Colossale, leans forward with a murmur of silk under pressure to retrieve the Journal and, having restored contact once more with his man of business, he settles facing the other way to await the next drive.

THE SPORTING COOK

There are ex-chalet girls who muck about with pasta, and there are sticklers who insist on giving you three courses, complete with frilly folded napkins when the keeper has ordered you back on your pegs in 45 minutes. There are some who suggest you might like a nice bit of salad and look startled when you stick a slice of Stilton into your mince pie. It's bit of a lottery to be honest and the roving Gun can expect to encounter all of these and more.

What a rare and particular pleasure it is then to encounter a sporting cook who really knows her stuff. Steak and kidney pud and mash, Shepherds Pie and peas. Mustard and tomato sauce on the table and not on demand. Chewy claret that had their necks knocked off at breakfast and have been standing on the mantlepiece over the roaring fire for the morning. A decent round of Stilton in the middle of the table. These are reassuring sights. Time is of the essence on a shooting day and simplicity is the friend of expedition. On a frosty January day the restoration of the inner Gun is a matter of piling in as much hot food as may be achieved in the time allowed. Everything therefore should be hot. Hot meat, hot veg, hot gravy, hot puds and lots of custard is the order of the day. Whereas, of course, the very reverse might be true after a blistering day at the partridges in September. Then cooling is king and a chilled soup, cold collation and a bucket of icy hock is called for. Followed by ice cream. And the cook is a queen among Guns who can deliver a sustaining lunch in a bothy high up on the moors in the middle of a sweltering day walking up the grouse. It is one thing to plonk yourself back on a shooting stick in December to let the delights of lunch subside, but here in the high tops strenuous exertion follows the break and the dyspeptic sensation of a jam roly-poly loitering about the waistband is no way to get the best out of the afternoon.

With experience comes wisdom. The ideal sporting cook has cooked for sporting households and, for that matter, may not be above taking her place in the line from time to time. She knows not only what is required to meet the needs of the day, but also that the way to a man's heart is through his stomach, and that a proper sporting repast will also provide the springboard for meeting the needs of the night. Not for nothing does the Royal McNab include the lodge cook, though on whose wall the trophy properly comes to rest is, more often than not, open to debate. There is a twinkle about the truly sporting cook, a secret ingredient, an understanding of the imperatives of the chase which lifts the spirits and stiffens the sinews and which no amount of recipe books and catering colleges can bestow.   Delicious.

THE GREAT SHE BEAR

She began picking up when her husband was still shooting. In those days ladies did not shoot, and to be honest she was blowed if she was going to mince about simpering all day. So she took herself off to the kennels and snagged herself a pup that no one else wanted. The pup was FTC Buckman of Swarbeam, founder of the Buckman strain, multiple winner of every prize on the circuit, saviour of babies in ponds and general all round wonderdog, known to his close friends as Scrap. Of course there will never be another like him, but one presses on regardless. She never has less than a half dozen in training, some her own and some for other people. She still has a soft spot for "problem" dogs and there is generally one in her string which has been delivered in despair. "Train it, keep it or shoot it!" tends to be the message. Generally she keeps it, trains it, wins several championships, and parts with it for a modest fortune. "The problem" she asserts firmly "is always with the owners. Hopeless, most of them. Quite hopeless." In fact the only thing which is more hopeless than most owners is the Kennel Club, the principals of which have a special place in her considerable and descriptive vocabulary.

For the dogs however, nothing is too good. For all she insists that they are working animals and she doesn't approve of pets, and despite the fact that they are fed on nothing more than the fallen stock which she shares with the hunt kennels, and notwithstanding that she is a lady both feared as well as honoured from one end of the country to another, a glimpse of the house or the car tells a different story. There are dogs everywhere. No sofa is sacred, no bed cover unmarked. Only the kennels themselves seem not to carry the scars of extensive use by dogs. Dog hair, dog toys, dog smell, dog leads, dog dummies, dog paraphernalia, dog junk, and dogs themselves lie about the house like the fallout from so many dog bombs. Somewhere in the midst of which is the husband whose reckless comments started the whole thing off four decades ago and who has never really recovered from the shock of confronting what he let out of the bottle. He can usually be found in the study - a moderately dog free zone - doing the crossword, practising bunker shots into the wastepaper basket and wondering how things would have turned out if he'd given her a nice set of irons as a wedding present and not suggested driven grouse as a honeymoon.

There are, for that matter, sundry children floating about. Not that it seems to matter terribly much. Given that they lived on an early diet of Bonios and were treated more or less the same as the latest batch of puppies they haven't turned out too bad. Not Championship material, you understand, but pretty decent all round working kids; housebroken, of course, and biddable. And dog bonkers, of course, which is all to the good. Can't imagine where they get it from.

GAME FAIR ~ FRIDAY

He walks the dogs early and then puts them in their run for the day. Then he bathes and changes and takes the old stick her early morning cuppa. While he is doing a quick check on the demesnes and policies she puts the final touches to the lists of jobs for the indoor and outdoor staff. Then it is into the motor and away before the hoi-poloi are stirring. Zoom down the motorway, cut through a couple of back ways that he's checked on the Ordinance Survey and straight into the Members Car Park on the dot of 0830 hours. A flash of badges and they're off and running before the dew has dried on the grass in the park. They've been doing it for decades and the routine is as effective today as it has always been. They are the Friday Fair Folk. County. To the core. Pips and juice, for that matter. She is in wafty silks and sensible shoes with a broad hat and a cardy round her shoulders and a pac-a-mac in her Tanner Krolle, just in case. He is in mufti; that's blazer and twill to you, with hunt buttons, regimental tie and a proper folding Panama hat with Varsity college colours hatband and a hole at the front where he has worn it out raising it to the ladies like a gentleman should. His brogues shine like well buffed conkers. They always come on Fridays to avoid the crowds and because all their friends come on Fridays to avoid the crowds too. Friday is a social event therefore in the same vein as Ladies Day at Ascot, though without the television people and the ghastly foreigners.

It is also however a day for renewing subscriptions, the airing of considered opinions, a certain amount of current and future shopping and then lunch. Accordingly breakfast is taken in the Game Conservancy, where the latest research on the grey partridge can be mulled over with a coffee and a croissant and the perennial issue of raptor control can be forcefully underlined. He's a life member here but next it is down to the Shooting Gazette to roll the sub and to chaff the girls and collect the free bottle of sloe gin. A scoot down Gunmakers Row demonstrates what everyone knows which is that all the top names have gone to the dogs and there hasn't been a decent gun built in this country since the war. And speaking of dogs, there is just time to catch the international retriever team trial for an hour before lunch. "Why can't your dogs be like those, dear?" "Because you will let them on the sofa and feed them biscuits, my love, that's why." Oh, well. And into the CLA for lunch. "Hello. How nice. Oh, yes, we've seen them too. Pimms? Do join us. Marvellous. Bigger and bigger, but Friday is still sort of the same, isn't it, I always think?" The afternoon is for shopping. Wellingtons and a new cap for him; half a dozen Tattershall check shirts at a giveaway show-special price, perhaps a new trout rod and a sports coat every fifth year. For her cashmere, new cardy and matching pashmina – "Well, I don't care what you call it, old thing, it's a wrap to me." – and a carrier bag of useful Christmas presents for those really difficult people that you can never quite find anything right for anywhere else. And into the Countryside Alliance for tea. It's all changed, of course, since the old BFSS days. All pretty girls and marketing now, though credit where credit's due, they did give those arses in Westminster a bloody nose with the march. Damn good day. Went up on the coach, both of us, at crack of sparrow's. Bloody Mary's all the way there. Lunch in the club. Whisky all the way home. Don't know what good it did, but damn good day anyway. Saw ever such a lot of people. Well done. Cheerio!

Then back to the car and away the way they came. No queues. No fuss. Rock solid. County. Proud of it. And so they should be.

GAME FAIR ~ SATURDAY

He's done a bit of alright, has Jeremy, and what with the bit of alright he's done he has accumulated this house in the country as a consequence. You know the sort of thing. Honeyed sandstone and Collyweston roof. Barns for the Jag XK and Tilly's little Beamer and, of course, the Disco for weekends. Paddocks for the ponies and a sit-upon mower which all their city friends just love playing with. The Aga's a given, naturally, though they have a hob and a microwave in their Smallbone country kitchen too because Tilly really hasn't quite got the hang of Aga cooking just yet. Any more than Jeremy has the hang of entertaining. "I mean what is the point of having this great place in the country if not for entertaining at weekends?" Well, yes. Certainly; but it probably helps if you remember to tell the distaff side that you have invited them. "What's the big deal, sweets? It's just the Carnforths and Tim and Belinda. Well, of course the children are coming. Can't they all muck in together? Just shoot into Tesco's and it will take care of itself. I'm sure they will bring stuff anyway. And we can get a burger or something at the Fair and then have dinner out if you really can't cope. Of course we'll find a babysitter. Whatsername? Works in the village shop. Has it? When? Really, darling? Still, I'm sure we'll find someone. Oh, I think I may also have invited Bobby and Val." And Tilly has a weekend for ten with seven children between eight and fifteen months, no food, the Labrador on heat and a Game Fair picnic to manage at short notice. It's the country house dream gone to Fulham in a handcart.

They're easy to spot because they go on Saturday. They have to. Jeremy is at work in the City and doesn't get away till late, even on a Friday and the Carnforths and Tim and Belinda and their au pair and the children and their Labradors don't arrive until nearly midday on Saturday anyway. Then, of course, there is the traffic, so it is well into the afternoon by the time they are setting off round the stalls. The grand picnic has been abandoned in favour of a snatched hog-roast bap and as a consequence the children are fractious. This is not the sort of fair the kids had in mind anyway, there being no dodgems, no ghost train and no candy floss flat. Tilly forgot the sunscreen into the bargain and so the little brutes are pinking up nicely and will not sleep tonight for love nor money. They are easy to spot. There's Jeremy and Tim in matching, to all intents and purposes, polo-shirts, Lands End shorts and deck shoes. Jeremy has little Jessica on his shoulders and the baby on his front and Tim has his two pulling on either side. Tilly and Belinda are plugging along behind with the others in double buggies; three wheeler for Till's and McLaren for Bel's each with a lardbutt Labrador lashed to the handles. They haven't bought anything because "There's no point carrying loads of stuff when there's so much more to see and we can get it later anyway." which they can't because they will never pass this stand again on their Ice Cold in Alex trans Saharan trek and if they did they would not know what to buy because they don't really understand what all this stuff is for, actually. Jeremy would like a gun, of course; but since his shooting has been limited to a corporate hostility outing where he borrowed everything except his Barbour, he is far from sure what the difference is between Boss, Beretta, Bosis, Browning, Baikal, Bazookah and Bofors and is too worried about showing it to ask. Also his collar is chafing and little Jess has peed down his neck. The country life is not turning out to be everything they promised in the brochure and he may just have to sue.

GAME FAIR ~ SUNDAY

Piece of cake, mate. Nike trainers, viscose running shorts, Claysport-Pro waistcoat in fluorescent yellow and black with the club logo across the shoulders over cammo singlet and multifarious tattoos. No.1 all over clip – head and chest - and a gold bracelet the size of Madagascar. An elderly spaniel on one side and a straining Dobermann on the other, maybe a bull terrier. Two kids at foot. Crewe, being where he was conceived, right? on the one hand in cargo pants, cammo T and a baseball cap who is disgruntled because Dad won't buy him the Cheyenne River 100% genuine 15" Bowie knife he has set his heart on. "I've told you, Crewe, you have to earn a knife like that. You don't just order it like pizza, mate. Get a job. Deliver something." And Kylie who is a tiny vision in pink. Pink trainers, pink hotpants, pink boob tube, pink eyeshadow, very pink shoulders and pinker still knees, pink lipstick, pink earrings, pink hair. And her not yet double figures. After a respectable top ten place in the open shoot it is time, come Sunday tea, for Dad to do some serious shopping and catch up with a few of the better bargains as the exhausted standholders are beginning to cash up and think of a day off after 72 hours straight of retail frenzy. There's a tasty Miroku 32" trap gun that he's had his eye on since the first morning down Gunmaker's where there is probably a deal to be done by now. A new shooting suit to be ordered before he leaves, for the invitations that very often follow a successful month's loading on the moors in the summer. And he needs a couple of nice sporting prints for the new conservatory and maybe a big old oil of partridges flaring across a

hedge for the mantle. Her at home needs something nice in silk, maybe, and while Crewe may be moping over the denial of his god given right to a lethal machete he will be pleased as punch with the nice little starter 20 bore that he will be getting for his birthday if his grades are alright at the end of term. The outlaw's Christmas presents always come from the Game Fair, as a matter of course, because he wouldn't be seen dead shopping anywhere else and there's a picture of Nev all tangled up in his cartridge belt to the life at Wossisname, the cartoonist's stand, which is just bound to be a snip for cash money by now and would look perfect in the lunch room of their little shoot in Essex. Lovely. And he always buys two pairs of dealer boots at the Fair because he gets through a pair a year on the lorries and another tramping round the sites. They are by no means the price they used to be when he first started coming to these shows as a lad, but he's been coming for so many years now that he's a known face these days and there's usually another discount for notes, if you know what he means? The missus used to come with him but got bored with two days of watching him shoot and he was not about to let her out alone here or she'd buy the place flat the first day, what with wood burners and pots and pans and that, so now she stays home and looks forward to a week in Spain as a consolation prize before he leaves for the moors on the Twelfth. "Never judge a book by its cover, mate"; and he should know, it's written in a nice curve across his back. Tasteful like.

BLACK POWDER HOUND

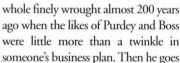

It is not inevitable that he has mutton-chop whiskers and a more than usually elaborate shooting suit and yet and at the same time it is not unlikely either. The chances are that there may be more than a hint of whisker and that the tweed check might be more than somewhat pronounced. A natty homburg hat and spats may not be out of the question and who is not the better off for that? He is a genial sporting cove. He is the Black Powder Hound. There is no great performance as he takes his place in the line and yet there is about him a sense of formality, almost of ceremony, as he begins what he describes as "setting out his stall". The rest of us shamble to our pegs and dump cartridge bags and sleeves on the grass. Dogs are settled and sat and even screwed down for the duration. The occasional shooting stick is planted. The Powder Hound has a table, well, a flat top on a stake, which he pushes firmly into the turf. Onto this go his powder flask and shot pottle, a little tin of percussion caps and then there is a box of waxed wads. Next to the table, thrust into the ground, are his ramrods – one for each barrel so that having duly rammed home a load in the one he can leave the rod there while he charges the second in order not disastrously to double load either. Dangling from about his person are his worm screw for unloading unfired charges and his nipple pin about which there has been much predictable merriment in the Guns' wagon on the way to first stand.

Having once set out the wherewithal the Hound proceeds to unship the smokepole with which he is going to undertake the day. On this occasion it is the 19 bore by Manton which slides from the sheepskin glowing dully brown in the sunshine. Brown stock of finest walnut and brown barrels of best Damascus the whole finely wrought almost 200 years ago when the likes of Purdey and Boss were little more than a twinkle in someone's business plan. Then he goes through the ritual of charging his piece. Powder and rod and wad and rod and shot and wad and rod. Twice. A quick poke down the nipples with the needle and caps on. Hammers at the half cock and he's as ready as anyone for the first birds of the morning. The rest of us just go "Thunk. Thunk. Thud" which is not the same thing at all. He may sweep back his cape. Then the birds begin to move. The old hammers glide back to full cock under the thumbs and "WHOOOOOMMPPHHH!! WHOOOMPHHH!!" White smoke rolls forth from the muzzles and a shower of sparks heads skywards. A bird bounces on the sward behind him but he's already halfway through his reloading ritual. Powderandrodandwadandrodandshotandwadandrod. Leave the rod in for safety and powderandrodandwadandrodandshotandwadandrod. Rods out. It doesn't do to spit a pheasant on your ramrod after all. And caps and "WHOOOMPHHH!! WHOOOMPHHH!!" and powderandrodandwadandrodandshotandwadandrodinandpowderandrodandwadandrodandshotandwadandrodandrodsoutandcaps WHOOOMPHHH!!WHOOOMPHHH!!-powderandrodandwadandrodandshotandwadandrodinandpowderandrodandwadandrodandshotandwadandrodandrodsoutandcaps. And relax. By which time all that can be seen of the Black Powder Hound is a huge cloud of white smoke loitering about his peg from which he emerges in due course at the whistle with a face covered in black soot, a broad grin you couldn't remove without a chisel and his homburg on fire. "I'm sure I got the first one" he says "but did anyone see if I hit anything after that?"

THE SHOOTING INSTRUCTOR

Young or old; boy or girl; novice or not; the one thing you have been taught since you were old enough to dribble on Granny's knee is to be safe. "Never, never let your gun pointed be at anyone." "Never point a gun at anything you don't mean to kill." "Never, ever point your gun….." and so on and so forth and so following ad nauseam and beyond. And the first thing that the Instructor invites you to do is shoot him straight between the eyes. The fact that when you do so, carefully unloaded and demonstrated to all and sundry to be so, natch, your barrels are pointing somewhere over his left ear and your right eye is watering with the effort of focusing on a bead that gives every appearance of being located on the end of his nose gives him the teeniest insight into why you have not been, are not, are never likely to be, connecting with either your usual or eagerly anticipated precision. Fit. Fit. Fit. Instructors are first and foremost tailors. Yes they can teach you to shoot, and to shoot well. And they are usually good shots, even great shots themselves; but first what they have to do is put eye and gun and shot in the same direction and into the same universe. And like a good tailor they are universally almost terminally solicitous. "Sir is putting his waistband under rather more pressure than once he was?" "Sir is tending to mount rather more hurriedly than is strictly necessary for the soaring archangel?" "Sir is tending to tension in the seat, methinks?" "Sir is flailing forlornly after an arse shot first barrel perhaps?" Indeed Sir is, and Sir wants it fixed pronto, before he makes a fool of himself in open court, if you please. And has Sir ever considered what effect bunging a damp gun into a wet sleeve at the end of the day and then driving it for a couple of hours in the superheated atmosphere of the executive limo might have on a slender and tensed and ever so slightly off centre sliver of fine French walnut? Like Sir, it relaxes and as a consequence ends up pointing somewhat in the wrong direction.

And once that is fixed we can get on with the meat of the thing which is the shooting and in shooting the principal objective is to bring shot and target tumultuously together and that means putting the shot ever so slightly ahead of the target; which means "A little more lead." which is engraved in letters of fire a mile high in the forefront of every instructor's brain and in the pupil's apparently nowhere.

And under an hour of his calm and encouraging influence we begin to hit unfeasible targets again and again while he murmurs soft words of congratulation into our shell-likes and for a brief and glorious moment we are super-Gun; elegant and stylish tidier up of the marginal bird behind our neighbour's neighbour. "I think that will do for now." says he, "Next time, perhaps, we can try something a little more challenging." And then you pays your money and emerge blinking into the real world.

YOUNG GUN

Shooting with the grown ups for the first time. Can ever so much pressure be heaped on young shoulders? "Be safe." "Be quiet." "Be polite." "Be safe." "Be modest." "Be smart." "Be safe." And more Be's besides. A positive swarm humming like supercharged hormones about his young head which is already spinning with excitement at the thought. There may have been walks with the keeper. There may have been outings with the old man after a pigeon and sundry armed marauds about the boundaries with the keeper, the tractor driver and Uncle Tom Cobleigh. There may have been solitary nights in the duck hide at half term in the faint hope of an occasional bang and a mallard carried home in triumph. And lessons at the shooting school besides. But this is the first day in the line with the grown ups. For all they are a carefully selected line of grown ups - including the aforesaid old man, sundry uncles and Godfathers and a sprinkling of those friends of the folks, who are betwixt and between and who often pitch up for weekends, but who are neither blood relative nor moral guardian, and who therefore have no proper title. Too irresponsible and fun to be called Mr. Whatever. Too old and aloof to be called Tom or Dick or Harry by a teenager. Let alone Pongo, Stinker or Biffy. Problems, problems, problems. Safe. Safe. Safe. Whatever you call them, there is not one who will be backward in tearing you off a strip if confronted by your muzzles across the line.

Draw for numbers like everyone else, amidst much comment about Uncle Jack and Pongo not getting a

shot off between them. Stifle a blush that is already surging about the new collar like a tidal wave. Drive with father to the first drive. He says as the engine stutters to a halt "Just relax. And be safe. " Feel about as relaxed and safe as a bishop in a bordello, and twice as likely to go off unexpectedly. Arrive at peg and unship trusty twenty. Dump bag of shells by slip and undo coat better to reach the still stiff birthday cartridge belt. Wait with cartridges in hand for the whistle before loading. Everyone is watching. Waiting for the first mistake. Of course they are. They are not thinking about pheasants, or partridges, or how they might have overdone the red infuriator a bit last night, or the new girl in the office, or whether it is the nephew's birthday this week. They are all like coiled springs waiting to pounce on the first error. 'S'obvious. That's why they're here.

Whistle goes; shells in. Relax. Pry fingers off fore-end. Don't click the safety like that. Fingers well away from triggers. Don't click the safety. Breathe. Occasionally. Gun is not a Black Mamba that needs strangling. Blink. "Over! Over left!" Oh God! A pheasant. Coming. Flying. Shoot it Uncle Jack. Pongo? Please. Yours. Mine. Oh Lord. Mount. Feet. Hands. Safety. Pull through. Blot and bang. OHMYGODDIDIGETIT?DIDI?DIDI?DIDI?

Thump.

"Nice shot." says Uncle Jack.

"Well done." says Pongo.

Suppress urge to gallop off to fetch bird. A flush of triumph suffuses cheeks.

"I should breathe now if I were you." says Uncle Jack.

THE LADY SHOT

When her late husband, bless him, not the latest late one, but an earlier late one, asked what she wanted as a wedding present she never hesitated for a moment. "Boss….." she said and that was all he needed to hear. She might have meant boscage in reference to the front garden or indeed Boston, Mass. for the honeymoon on Cape Cod; but the upshot was a nice pair of sixteens which she uses today with no less effectiveness and delight than the day they arrived - Oh, more years ago than she cares to remember, or you to ask, if you know what's good for you.

She has many skills, and if you look at the wedding photographs, the early ones….well, any of them actually, you will recognise that she had, has had, has still much else besides. Her only failing seems to have been losing husbands. Admittedly if they lead from the front storming things in whatever war is current, hunt three days a week, and big game at that, and drive fast cars fast at weekends while living on a diet of red meat, whisky and cigars there is a tendency towards early departure. Still, live fast, die young, shed a tear and move on. All girls want today is a flat, a job and a pension. Don't know they're born.

Still, along the way the husbands provided sufficiently in many respects. The moor though she brought with her as a dowry - each time - and it remains her pride and joy. She knows it probably better than she knew any husband, but then she has had it longer. And God help any keeper or guest who can't keep up with her as she pounds about after the grouse in summer or the stags in the autumn - or for that matter the hinds in deepest winter. She and her stalker are legends on the hill both together and separately and stories abound concerning their forays after the hinds in the corries in the snow.

She is formidable on the low ground too. Quite apart from her manifest skill and the fact that her invitation both back and forth has been an annual event for the best part of two generations already, she is good company and a wise counsel. Her stories can bring a tint to the cheek of the most hardened beater. Many a young keeper has benefited from her brief comments following this drive or that, and many an old keeper, for that matter, has bathed in her compliments and the congratulations of others, having put her advice into practice. She has a knack for spotting where birds will go that comes with years of experience, and will often mooch a few yards off her peg at the end of a line of Guns to act as unofficial stop by the corner. Not that so doing will stop her reaching out and demolishing that soaring archangel that her neighbour has just given up on as being too, too high.

She's no slouch indoors either, actually, and while she can convulse the company with charades after her dram, it would be a brave man who played her ton-up in the billiards room for a quid a point, regardless of the time of day. They say that it would take a brave man to let her name the stakes, as a matter of fact, or the game, when the candles and the decanter are low enough at the end of a shooting day. They say. Men today! Boys! Don't know they're born.

THE LOOSE CANON

Time was when every country parson was a regular on the shoot. Now he's a rarity and even a brace of birds left with the best will in the world on the rectory steps will be met with dismay rather than thanks. There are still a few sporting clergy out and about though. The Loose Canon can be relied upon to pick-up through the season. He has a brace of springers who are sound either in the beating line or behind the Guns and he is a shoe-in for the keeper's day. Or for a foreshore flight of a morning come to that. The elderly Volvo has seen service these many seasons past and the barrels of his old Webley are worn almost silver with the years, but he can still pull down the occasional archangel when the opportunity presents itself, although he would be the last to refer to a high bird as an archangel. "We're on the same side, after all," he chortles, "and the boss wouldn't want me shooting the staff, now would he?" His dog-collar can be seen peeping through the woolly scarf that was made for him by one of his elderly parishioners and the crook he leans on while he gets his pipe going is as much a tool of his Saturday recreation as it is a symbol of his Sunday work. He's always happy to take a brace of birds at the end of the day as part of his reward for his labours and is not above offering up a short prayer at the start of the day which recognises the joys of the sport to come, or indeed a word or two of thanks at the end, as he stands beside the game-cart.

He even says grace before delving into his gamebag for his lunchtime sandwich, can of ale and the hefty doorstop of fruit-cake. Then it is out with the thermos and his tobacco pouch and a quick canter through the Times crossword before the first drive of the afternoon. His fund of sporting reminiscences is abundant and his jokes in the beaters' wagon are legendry. His sermons are littered with sporting references and while he no longer hunts, the hounds are always welcome to meet at the rectory where there is a glass of port or a sloe gin ready for the huntsman and the followers and he is a fixture at the Boxing Day meet with a box of mince pies in one hand and his capacious flask in the other. "The Lord giveth," as he says, "but the Master taketh away!" Nor does his sporting instinct diminish with the close of the formal season. He can be relied upon to take a stand in the copse at the foot of the rectory garden during the roost shooting in February and is a regular in the middle of a decoy pattern on the young beans. Decoying, he says, combines the best of both worlds: the opportunity to shoot on the one hand and time to think about Sunday's sermon while sitting in the midst of God's creation, on the other. Although he has never succumbed to the lure of wedded bliss, his is not a life without company. After his dogs, his other passion is for his ferrets and the loose-boxes beside the rectory are filled with hutches. The sight of the Volvo parked up some lane beside a likely looking hedge is a common enough site round the parish. And the neighbouring parishes come to that, for his renown as man who can be relied upon to make an impact on the rabbit population is widespread and there is no shortage of invitations to ply his skills on the estates round about.

The sporting parson is indeed a rarity these days, and possibly endangered, but where sport and spirituality still meet, there will be the Loose Canon still.

THE STOP

He has a spot for every drive; and every drive has its spot. Sometimes the spot is natural and sometimes he has to create it with a long sewelling line. Tha's hus job, tha' us. He en't a keeper or a brusher. He dun't flank and he dun't pick up less'n that old bud jes' fall in hus lap. He's a Stop. Tha's hus job. And he's being doing it from the year dot and he knows to the minute, to the second, to the breath when the moment has come. To do what exactly? To Stop. On the first drive, for example, the birds will all be congregated in the east end of the Long Spinney. Because that is where they are fed every morning early by the keeper and where they congregate to soak in the first early rays of the warming sun. And then they amble back up the hedge towards home in the deep heart of the big wood. That's where they live. Only this morning they have got to earn their living by taking a spin across the Guns. The keeper fed at or about first light as usual and by 7.15am there was a goodly congregation of pheasants getting stuck into the corn in the feed rides through the Long Spinney. By 7.45am they were beginning to edge back towards the hedge and a brisk walk home. Only they were Stopped. There's no great magic to Stopping. It's not loud and it's not heavy handed. In fact it is very much a matter of being there. In the right place; at the right time. Just as the birds thought they might be getting along, there he was. Sitting on the fallen oak in the yellow reflective council issue donkey jacket which betrays his weekday job spinning the Stop/Go sign for the road repair teams and battered bobble hat, sipping tea from his thermos and rolling the first of the day. And whistling through his teeth. So the pheasants draw back into Long Spinney and have a bit of a conflab about the whole situation and then they send out a couple of scouts who report in due season that he's still there and time is getting on. But the pheasants, while they may be creatures of habit are not rigid adherents to regimen and Long Spinney is warm and the sun is agreeable and there is still grain in the straw. So they wait awhile. And he's still there. This time they make a more determined effort to get past him and several emerge from the spinney together at which the Stop hefts to his feet and says "Hoy!" and taps his boot with his withy and the pheasants scurry back inside once more. And so it goes on until just after 9.15 when one of the beaters is sent to relieve him. And he takes himself off with stern warnings to the lad to "Keep them buds in 'ere anither five minutes. I've 'ad 'em thur best past of two hurs and Ah dun't want yew buggerin' it all up now!" And he plods off down the hedge to the end of the next drive where he has already stretched his sewelling across the brow of the slope and even as he slides his back down the trunk of the broad beech to hunker comfortably at its base the first shots are carried to him on the breeze and a cock emerges from the brambles to find the Stop hissing at him "Gebbeck y'old bugger. I aren't a'ready fer yer yit!" and the cock slips back down through the brush with the news that the obvious line of retreat from the beaters who are already lining out along the far edge of the wood seems to be interrupted by a curtain of twitching shredded fertiliser and feed bags and what is that all about exactly?

And sometimes he merely stands behind a tree. Now in the open, now in shadow. Now you see him, now you don't. Now a whistle, there a tap. And the birds flush in ones and twos. They are uncertain but not startled. Their heads are up as they look about and lift into the air, not cowed and scared, and they fly high as the consequence and handsome and the keeper is congratulated and duly rewarded at the end of the day. But he will see the Stop right later for sure, because without him the shooting day would be like trying to hold water in a paper bag. He's the Stop. Tha's whut he dew. Tha's hus job. Jes' Stoppin'.

THE PROFESSIONAL

He arrives in a truck with a positive pack of dogs in the back; but do they teem out like lemmings as soon as the door is open? Is the Pope a Presbyterian? No, they sit in a row, bright eyed and alert waiting for the word or the snap of the fingers that unleashes them. Sometimes only half the tide responds to the word, or as it might be the snap; the other half staying rooted to the spot until their personal signal is given. Then they assemble in a neat semi-circle at the feet of the master.

No leads here. No choke chains or hard words. Just unquestioning, adoring obedience. Except for the pup on the one hand who has much to learn but is coming on in leaps and bounds and the oldest member of the team to whom a special licence is given to behave somewhat more like a normal dog and to seek out the smells and excitements of a shooting morning.

During a drive the team variously sit or lie behind the line watching the shooting and marking down the birds as they fall. When a pelleted cock bounces once, gathers himself and legs it for the nearest hedge a dozen eyes flick from the bird to the boss and back again, imploring. Ooh Sir. Me Sir. Pleessir. Meesir. Please. "Tess!" says the master and, like a streak of gold, or as it might be black, Tess leaves a trail of scorched earth in her wake while the remainder stay rooted to the spot with a mixture of envy and disappointment in their expressions. Upon her return with a still lively bird, the chosen one delivers it to hand without any of the circling or creeping of a lesser retriever. She comes, she sits, she offers up the bird and releases it without a struggle. Then she resumes her place in the row of dogs. Job done.

When the shooting is over the pup is dispatched for the dead bird nearest by. At the same time another is sent for the long bird which towered beyond the fence. "Giddout!" and a flick of the fingers is all the direction he needs. The dog knows what he's about. And he has the trophies at home to prove it. The fence might just as well not be there as he clears it by a foot or more and is onto the bird in less time than it takes to tell. Back across the obstacle with one wing across his eyes, but that makes not a jot of difference, there is no hesitation. Then home, sit, offer up, a pat and sit down. The pup is having a problem getting the whole of her bird into her mouth. Eventually, after spitting out a couple of feathers, she gathers it up and potters somewhat tentatively back. On arrival she forgets to sit, and has her bottom grounded and is made to wait, unrelieved of her burden while another dog is sent into the lake for the bird that is floating yonder. Once he is en route with a spectacular flying entry the master turns once more to the pup and relieves her of her bird and praises her extravagantly. Finally the last pair are dismissed to clear the ground of any remaining birds and then they will sweep round behind the Guns to check for birds overlooked by less diligent or skillful teams.

Can it really be like this? Always? Without fail? Where are the japes, the antics, the tantrums and the plain bloody mindedness that inform the relationships of the rest of us with our dogs? In the past, is where. In the past. Amateurs have anecdotes, professionals have prizes. That's the difference.

THE BEATER'S DOG

Is inevitably a spaniel. Springer for choice. And confused with it. The confusion runs thussish. "Listen, mate: you want me to hunt for pheasants. There are pheasants in this bramble bush. You know it and I know it. The pheasants certainly know it. So, if I go in this end, and I will – I'd love to. I can't wait. I mean, did you ever see a more prickly and savage bramble bush? Stands to reason it's stuffed with pheasants, right? – so if I go in this end and scramble and squeeze through along the ditch underneath, all the pheasants, and there are pheasants in here, believe me, there are pheasants, I know, I can smell them from here, hordes of them, squadrons, mate, flotillas of pheasants, they're all going to come flying out the other end, right? and you are going to be a fat lot of good standing there with your little stick, ain'tch'a? On the other hand, experience dictates that if I rush in there, and I will, soon, now, almost immediately, if not sooner, instead and grab one by the arse and drag it back out here, - which is the object of the exercise, after all, right? Bird in hand better than two in bush, right? Fetch? Retrieve? That sort of thing? – I know you're going to go peculiar about it. So the question is, boss, how come on any given day hunting pheasants is good and on most days bringing them back is better but on some days you get so aerated about the fact and go all squeaky? I mean, I'm only asking? Forget it, I'm going in. This is just too good to miss. I'll be back later. Probably. Maybe. We'll talk. Later. Byeeee! Hello pheassie friends. C'mon boys. Papa's home!" Mad, of course. Whoever invented the term "Barking mad" probably owned a spaniel. "Ooooh! Look! A freezing ditch with ice round the edges! Yeeeaahhhh! Look at me, dad! Look at me! I'm swimming! Wait a second. What's that? Hey, unless I'm very much mistaken there could be little phezzie wezzie holed up just under this bank. Hold the phone, boss, I'm definitely getting something down the old schnozzeroonie. Lookit. Just…..in….here! Goddim! 'Ell, 'on't 'ust 'and 'ere! 'Ive us a 'and. I've 'ot a right 'outhful 'ere! 'Ot a 'loody 'ell 'ou 'ean "Let go"? Are we 'unting 'loody pheasants or what? Oh, alright. There. What? Oh now you've changed your mind? Now you want the damn thing caught again? Well, catch it yourself, matey. I'm off into these thorny bushes. When you've made up your mind whether you want these birds caught or not or just chased about or retrieved you give me a whistle. OH, HOW PERFECTLY FANTASTIC! THERE'S SOMETHING IN HERE THAT'S BEEN DEAD FOR MONTHS!! I'll just have a quick roll and then you can have a whiff of it later when we get home and I've warmed up a tad. Mum'll just love that, don't you think? Can we go swimming again, dad? Can we? Can we? Can we? HARE!!!! MINE!!! Leave it to me!! I'm on it!! OK. OK. OK. Not to chase the hares. Or the rabbits. OK. OK. I said OK. I forgot, right. Momentary lapse. OK? Don't go on so. OW!!WHATTHEHELLWASTHATFOR?GOPICK ONSOMEONEYOUROWNSIZEWHYDON'T YOU! SORRYSORRYSORRYsorrysorrysorry!

Hey! Will you just take a look down this pit? Brambles and an icy pond! Oh, can I go and take a look, dad? Can I? Can I? Wheeeeee! PHEASANTS!!"

All day long. Day in, day out.

ROUGH SHOOT

The captain of the rough shoot wants to manage Blenheim. Or Burghley; or Belvoir. Or Miltons. Or Molland; or Middleton. What he's got is 250 acres in and about Piddlehampton and a sort of licence to trespass in pursuit of game on the Eight Acre behind the forestry in exchange for many pints for the keeper next door unless his boss happens to be watching. The Guns at Blenheim or Burghley or Belvoir are either immensely wealthy guests from America or the Middle East who arrive in helicopters and fleets of blacked out Range Rovers with liveried loaders and pickers-up and crocodile skin gun cases. At Piddlehampton the Guns are the seed merchant who half inches most of the grain for the birds, two neighbouring farmers whose goodwill is essential to the shoot's survival, the barman at the pub who does lunch in lieu of his sub, the two oldest members who sort of came with the territory and the local doctor which is a bit of a boon because the way some of the older members shoot there could be an urgent need for surgery at any time. In fact given the advanced age and questionable health of the older members there could be any amount of calls on the doctor's time if something really exciting happened. Like a flush. The keepers at Miltons or Molland or Middleton are dapper and deferential in estate tweed and each has an immaculate brace of retrievers at foot and fifty drilled and regimented beaters at their beck and call. The keeper at Piddlehampton is Derek who does shifts on the lorries and fits in some feeding in and around his proper job. His real delight in keepering is to zoom round the farm on his quad bike in the middle of the night with a million candlepower lamp and a positive arsenal of weaponry executing foxes at unfeasible distances. The beaters on the great estates are recruited from the tenant farms and know the signature drives almost as well as the beatkeepers from long experience in different conditions. They do not yell or holler but maintain a steady tap-tap-tap and their dogs quarter the brambles and undergrowth no more that a few paces ahead of the line. The beaters at Piddlehampton are less recruited than press-ganged. There are several children of varying ages most of whom should probably be at school anyway and who belong either to the Guns or to Derek or to other beaters. The rest are usually to be found in the pub. Wives at Piddlehampton do not stand decorously and decoratively on the pegs with their spouses but are driven with spurs and goads and unlikely promises into the undergrowth. Dogs career here and there unrestrained, giving tongue now and again as they course deliriously after rabbits and leggy cocks. In the event of game being sighted the entire beating line erupts into a chorus of whoops and cheers and cries of "Forward!" "Back!" and "Look! There! A whatsit thingummy! Pot it someone!" A single, definitive "Bang!" elicits a great cheer. A double bang inevitably provokes a chorus of jeers and snatches of "Why was he born so beautiful……?" At pukka shoots the pickers-up focus on the birds pricked during the drive to begin with and then move steadily forward after the horn collecting and despatching as they go until they finally mingle with the Guns by their pegs saying "Take that for you, sir?" and "Yes, I have that one, Sir." At Piddlehampton any bird that hits the deck is pounced upon by any number of dogs and not a few children who then argue vociferously about who saw it first until Derek beats them back with a stick and salvages the remains. The bag at Molland or Miltons or Middleton may run into hundreds, but at Piddlehampton they are happy if the bag outnumbers the Guns. But they are happy. Except the captain who still wants to manage Blenheim or Burghley or Belvoir. More fool him probably.

LIKE A MILITARY OPERATION

He says nine-fifteen for nine-thirty, but he means 0900 hours for 0907, given that a kettle takes four minutes to boil, if watched, and the resulting coffee will take six minutes to cool to an average 68° in order to be drinkable by an average human being; which leaves three minutes to make the brew-up and ten to swallow it assuming average pace being maintained all round. OK? This means that the first drive can be blanking in at 0845, on the basis that the birds will congregate in the pines at 0925 and can be held there by the stops for ten minutes only which requires us to be on our pegs and ready at 0935 for a first flush at approximately 0936.30. Right. Any questions?

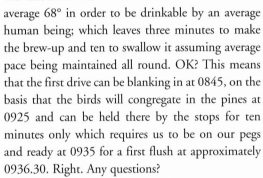

Perhaps he was an artillery commander before he accumulated the estate, and perhaps whole regiments depended for their very lives on the split second timing of his salvoes, fusillades and barrages; but do I really need this now? Quite often, it has nothing whatever to do with military training and much to do with some management consultancy course that pointed out that you should always hire the candidate with the tidiest desk. This guy sharpens his pencils of an evening in order to leave the morning free for really important tasks like polishing his stapler.

Now it is perhaps unnecessarily cruel to pick on the generalissimo in this way. He has after all invited us, or at least let us on the place under whatever terms and conditions; but he has forgotten the central issue rather, which is that the day should, after all is said and done, be fun. And that is kind of difficult if you are being harried from pillar to post hither and yon, and being given wholly unintelligible instructions as to what to do when you get there.

"Follow the hedge-line up to the apex and stand 43 yards due south of the Arboris Giganticus at map reference 100985. After three minutes or 1031 hours, whichever is the later, move 80 yards East by magnetic North or away from the nearest beater. Don't whatever you do shoot before then or you will ruin everything. Understood?" In a pig's eye.

The principal difficulty he consistently overlooks is that we are dealing here with birds and animals and beaters and, to be frank - us. And few of the above will conform to the strict regimentation he is inclined to inflict. Especially after lunch. Chaos Theory dictates that the greater and more rigid the control that is placed upon fluid or organic entities, the greater their likely divergence from the plan once left to their own devices. More or less. Which means that the Guns are usually facing in the wrong direction behind the wrong hedge, the birds have all legged it down the ditch towards the spinney and the beaters are having a smoke in the wrong wood while waiting for the keeper to blow the whistle he has left at home down the walkie-talkie that the host has left on the dashboard of the game cart in the first place.

THE SPORTING AGENT

Is it any wonder that he is grey beyond his years, and wan with it? The Sporting Agent is a hostage. Not only to fortune, but also to either side of the sporting bargain. Basically, if anything goes wrong on the shooting day, it is his fault.

Too few birds – his fault. Too many – his fault. Guns not up to snuff – his fault. Guns at the wrong farmyard – his fault. Rain, wind, fog, snow, ice, sunshine – his fault. Claret too cold; Chablis too warm – all without exception his fault.

On top of which the Sporting Agent attends some ninety shoots a year and watches 750 Guns having a ball, and gets to take his own gun out on half a dozen occasions, usually crammed into the last week of the season to help mop up a few cocks before it is too late.

You have to ask why anyone would bother.

There is the money, of course. The fee for functioning as an honest broker between strapped shoot owners on the one hand and loaded and heavily armed parvenus on the other. A modest recompense for the introduction of the impecunious to the impervious.

Modest indeed when you see some of the teams who turn up. They send in a perfectly reasonable looking skipper who acts as a Trojan Horse and proceeds to unleash a pack of overexcited animals upon the unfortunate hosts, keepers and beaters. They arrive late with all the wrong equipment and loudly address the day from the off through a positive tidal wave of alcohol and mind enhancing

pharmaceuticals. They fusillade and salvo in all directions excepting, of course, towards the birds which are the object of the exercise, and by the time they retire to the house for lunch, most of the beating line are emerging from the woods on all fours and the pickers–up are still on the second drive hiding behind a stack of bales waving a hanky on a stick. The Sporting Agent must do something. Then the lunchtime entertainment arrives in a charabanc from Soho. It's all his fault.

Or, as it might be, the keeper is on strike, the beaters have been seduced away to the neighbouring estate, the pickers-up have broken down and the birds haven't been seen for a week. The cook has consumed the entirety of the lunchtime Lafite and has refilled all the decanters with Mateus Rose before passing out in front of the Aga which has blown up, leaving little more than some peanuts and a lump of what might be frozen something for lunch. And it's all his fault.

As the years pass, with experience comes wisdom. Teams and estates become regular, if occasional, partners and can for the most part be left to their own devices. But still new teams and new venues must be recruited to keep the whole operation staggering on and to keep the Sporting Agent in tweeds and claret. And every evening from August to February the Sporting Agent watches the telephone in case it should scuttle across the room and bite him. And it would still be his fault.

POWER BEHIND THE PEG

"Well this is nice, I must say. I can't remember the last time we stood together on your peg on a shooting day. When was it, do you suppose? Do you know I actually think it wasn't long after we were married? I think it's awfully nice of them to make such a point of asking the wives along. It makes for a much more rounded sort of a day, don't you agree? I can't imagine what it must be like if you are all just boys together. Whatever do you talk about? I mean it's not as if you have very much in common all of you, is it? What? Oh, cartridges. Yes, I've got them here. Just hold on while I get the bag organised. What do you mean you want some now? There aren't any pheasants about just yet are there? Oops! You're right, there's a few moving already. They don't usually come quite that quickly, do they? You always say that you can spend ever such a lot of the time just waiting. Well, don't hurry me; I've just got to get my gloves off so I can manage this buckle. I really don't know why they don't make these things with a nice clasp like a handbag. It would be ever so much easier. There look, I swear I've pulled a nail. Don't fuss so! I'm sure there will be some more along in a minute. Now there you go. What do you mean you want some more already? You haven't used those yet? Well, I'll be ready next time. You missed that one anyway. That one. Over there where David is standing. Oh, now he's shot it. Well, I think you could have got it even if it was his bird. You're always telling me what a great shot you are. You spend enough time at that shooting school after all. There you are. Don't blame me. I was holding it out. No, you pick it up. You dropped it. I'm not getting down on my hands and knees in this mud to look for your bullets if you can't just open your mitt and take the damn things. Take these then. What about that one? That one! Oh dear. Was that a miss then? Tush, dear! Language. Really, I don't care. Someone might hear you. It's only a pheasant after all. Ooh, quickly look! No; at Tim and Caroline. They seem to be having a bit of a tiff! How exciting! I've never understood how they came together in the first place. Do take a gander, darling. Tim's gone all red, you know the way he does. Bad luck! I think I saw some feathers come out though. Is that bad? Why? Surely you hit it though? Sorry. Here you are. Well, I didn't realise you'd fired them both, I was watching Tim and Caroline. What about this one? Well, it looks quite high enough to me and anyway you couldn't get the last one and that was no higher. Well, I think that's just silly. Whatever is the point of coming all this way and then just ignoring the poor things? Ooh, I say. Robert just got two right together. That's awfully clever, isn't it? Why couldn't Claire come with him this weekend? Gosh, he's just done it again. He must be frightfully good, mustn't he? Sorry, what? Oh, here. Damn this flap; it just won't stay open. Sorry! Here's one. This must be all right. Ooh I say, darling, you got it. Absolutely amidships! Look at all those feathers! And again, darling! Getting in the groove now, aren't we, poppet? Sorry, I was just watching that one. It seems to be not quite dead. No, it's walking off. Oh, the poor little thing. It's limping. Shall I run after it? Ooh no. I couldn't possibly. Perhaps I might just put my foot on it? Sorry! I rather lost track there for a moment. Here you are. Is that a horn? Oh, well that was exciting, wasn't it? Why do you think I should stand with Robert for a while? I thought he was doing rather well considering he's by himself. Well, if you really think he needs helping, of course I will. Are you sure you can manage without me? It would be nice to stand with someone who shoots quite so well for a change. Darling? Are you quite all right? Darling?"

AGRICULTURAL STUDENT

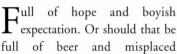

Full of hope and boyish expectation. Or should that be full of beer and misplaced anticipation? "Actually the course is, y'know, like really, really hard work. There's more agrono-momby...agromony.....agrobnomy...science and, y'know, accounts and stuff in it these days, y'know. And science was not my strong subject at school y'know. I was a full back. And adding up is like, well, y'know, fourteen of us tried to split a bill for dinner the other night and it took, like, forever. Yeh, I guess that is division, right, but, right, y'know, that's just the point, yeh? I'm taking it, you know, like really, really seriously because otherwise the old boy will, you know, never really trust me really to, you know, run things while he's around. And, y'know, I think I really have, like, plans for the place which will make serious dosh."

The old boy, meanwhile, has already made the decision to live forever in order to keep things ticking over on the farm at home and parking the principal heir and successor at the Royal College for a spell is only one of a long series of plans designed to keep the old homestead out of younger hands for decades to come. Fire him off to Oz or Argentina next. That should keep him occupied for a year. In his own day, of course, it was a quick and dirty stint spent drinking beer and chasing skirt and shooting pheasants and then straight into the estate office for the duration. Tried and tested four course rotation, cereals at hundreds the ton, the dairy washed its face

and more and the pheasants were slid through the farm accounts with never a word said.

The world is a harder place these days and while with some application and diligent management of Countryside Stewardship schemes, hedging grants, organic certification, barn conversions and permanent set-aside the arable can be kept hanging on by its fingernails, the dairy is now an expensive luxury and the pheasants are paid for by high rolling "shooting is the new golf" corporate hostility outings with scarcely a mooch about the boundaries for the family once in a blue moon.

The boy might as well have his fun while he can, because managing the caravan park and the PYO strawberry stall is no picnic and collecting the litter after a long bank holiday weekend in the Countryside Adventure Park is enough to make a farmer, if that is the right term, weep.

So let him drink beer and play rugby and polo and spin his clapped out Golf on the gravel and shoot the occasional pheasant with the last survivor of Grandpa's garniture of London guns from the days when farmers were gentlemen and vice versa and Grandpa's last surviving suit for that matter, and live the dream for a season. With any luck he will marry a lawyer, or a nice girl with one of the big consulting firms whose dad has a computer company and will end up in clover. Not that he'd recognise clover if he was ankle deep in the stuff. Which he won't be for a while.

91

THE MARCHERS

Mum and Dad and Auntie Glad, Uncle Fred and sister Jean and all the cousins in between; and here's a ferret and there's a horse; we left the hounds at home, of course.

And we may look like tourists, because for the most part that is exactly what we are; for the time being. But happen you don't want our horse-boxes on your pavements permanent, Tony matey, best you get your tanks out of our coverts.

And we shall all be there. Shoulder to shoulder. From portly Bufton Tuftons who may have to stop off at the club en route, via the farmer from the shires through the huntsman in the wolds to the shepherdess in the hills and the falconers in the valleys, from moorland keepers to highland stalkers and back again with gillies and whips and pickers-up in between and boots on. Farm, fur, feather and fin. Copse, covert, hedge, hill, moor, mere, lock, stock and flaming barrels. Everyone whose work, sport, hobby, interest, pursuit or recreation involves real earth, real things, real animals, real people, real stuff, will be there, here and now, to tell these, these, these, these… CREATURES, once and for all to BACK OFF.

United in a singleness of purpose that mealy mouthed politicians and their fawning acolytes can only dream of buying with greasy backhanders we shall demonstrate together to keep and to protect what generations have built up over centuries and which will not be wrenched away in an instant by vote-hungry timeservers with an eye to the main chance.

And while Mum and Dad and Auntie Glad, and all the tinies too, may variously be green and tweedy and puffa'd and jolly and red faced and honest and upright and weather beaten and gnarled and polished and red coated and booted and spurred and what-have-you'd to a picture postcard perfect caricature of ourselves, not so very deep down we are very, very angry.

And the politicians say "We're listening" "We're listening" "We're listening"

Well, – we were forced to march; but we're ready to fight. Listening is not good enough.

THE TERMINATOR

He prefers a rim-fire .22 for the rabbits, although you do have to upgrade the scope in order to compensate for the slight throw you sometimes get from the sound moderator. Of course, if you're lamping foxes you ought to be using a centrefire. Probably .225 or even a .243, although the latter is probably overdoing things a bit, unless you are principally a stalker that is, when the .243 will be the calibre of choice for obvious reasons. Unless the .270 is more to your taste. Or a crossbow. Did you know that the new graphite/kevlar bonded crosspiece Stealth II is capable of developing over 1,000 foot pounds of thrust when combined with a polypropylene/lycra blend string with a braided steel core? That's equivalent to almost 800 fps, which is like a short-barrelled Colt at close range? And it's driving a thing with the same dimensions as a .45 short changed wadcutter. Imagine!

For pigeons he likes a 7/8ths oz. Competition Load, because that extra metre per second is central to the clean kill on the second bird over the magnet. And you get the same speed with less muzzle flip with the 7/8ths than, say, the 1 oz Gold Pigeon. Always assuming you are using a side by side, that is. If you use an O/U for decoying, and a lot of people do, then muzzle flip is a non-issue because of the extra weight. But then the weight is what counts when you are decoying, because you may have to mount the gun hundreds of times during a session and that's why he prefers the lighter gun. Except when he takes out the 20 bore O/U; but then he would probably not use the 7/8ths with it, preferring, as he does, to settle for a 13/16ths Hi-Powa which gives him all the pace he needs and a good killing zone to boot. And it doesn't do your head in either.

And he's got a knife for skinning and a knife for whittling and a knife for cutting bits of string and binder twine. And he's got any number of tools in little leather pouches on his belt. This one is a complete set of interchangeable screwdrivers and that one combines with the attachments to make a socket set which would enable him to change the gearbox on a Range Rover should the chance arise, or to convert any standard petrol V8 to diesel in little more than an afternoon, which would amount to a cost saving of maybe 30p per litre or more if you convert to LPG; although LPG isn't as universal round here as it should be.

Not that being marooned without fuel would matter a tinker's cuss to him because with his waterproof, windproof lighter cum torch cum chainsaw he could survive on a desert island made only of volcanic rock for literally months with only what he has in the pockets of his Lo-Profile Kammo combat jacket which renders him invisible on everything from tundra to the birch woods of Arkansas.

And somehow, at some point, you find yourself wishing you were in either.

OUT OF SEASON GUN

Indoors. Out of Season. Out of Practice. And Out of Sorts. The season is three or four months gone. The pigeons are out of bounds for the time being. The shooting school is closed. And the Out of Season Gun is on the brink of picking spots of light off the wall and bottling them. Once you have taken the guns out of the cupboard for the umpteenth time to check that there is no rust on them from fingerprints you might have inadvertently left the last time you took them out to check, you should be aware that you are standing at the top of a precipitous and well greased incline and at the foot is the nuthouse. Or evening classes. If the community bobby took a shufti at most serious game shooters just about now, there would scarce be a Certificate in private hands come the grouse season. This is the time of year when even the budgie refuses to come out for a flitter round the drawing room without an escort and the guinea pigs hang out the Do Not Disturb sign.

The best thing to do is to take the guns to the smith for their annual overhaul, to get them out of the way for the time being. This is an outing, though, fraught with peril as the Out of Season Gun is unlikely to emerge from the gunshop without having added some additional little necessity to the Certificate – well, it's not often you actually have it with you, is it? When the fit is on? Best thing for the gun business the Feds. ever did, making folk cart their Certificates with them every time they pop out for a box of squibs. Bound to happen. Failing which there is always the new decoy/hide netting/ear-defenders/ knife/extractor/ hipflask/powder-flask/shotflask/ramrod/muzzleloader/little Boss 20 bore to contend with.

Go home. Read the Game Books. Think back and remember, remember that day in November when it all went just perfectly and the birds flew high, wide and handsome and you were pulling them down from all points of the compass with style and panache. This exercise should last you about four minutes, at least.

There is much to be said out of season for the humble air rifle. Quite apart from the actually visceral, simple satisfaction that may still be derived from reducing a perfectly ordinary soft drinks can to a colander, useful hours can be easily wasted stalking rats in the grain dryer or some such likely spot or taking after the squirrels, as it might be in the planting, or even in the garden. Patience and stillness are the key to success naturally. So it's not really going to cut the proverbial condiment. No; if the rapid discharge of huge quantities of ammunition for no discernible result is what lights your particular fire, and under these peculiar circumstances it is, really, isn't it? then the only healthy answer is to empty the holiday money pot beside clock on the mantelpiece and head down to the amusement arcade where for the price of a box of Bismuth shells you can do in any number of virtual video enemies and return home a more relaxed and amenable co-habitee. And they give you prizes.

THE COURT JESTER

There's usually one in every beating line. If you are lucky he will be a complete stranger, who will nonetheless be ready with a comment on the performance of the Guns in general. If you are unfortunate, he will know you as an individual and will take the mickey out of your personal performance throughout the day with more remorseless accuracy than you will be able to muster under the circumstances. "Well, well, Boys, now we shall see something. The finest team of game shooters in the country. Sorry, that's next week isn't it? So who have we here then? Har. Har. Har." And once it has started, you can be sure it will carry on all day. "What was wrong with that cock bird, lads?. Perhaps it was a stealth bomber then? Har. Har. Har." This is the beater who shouts "Over!" when the tail-less hen pheasant comes to you during the partridge drive, and gets you every time. This is the joker who calls "Back! Back!" when you are just in the middle of a quiet pee behind a tree after lunch. This is the commentator who asserts after the elevenses break that "I hope he's had a good pull at yon flask. He shoots a good deal better when he's had a decent gargle." thereby suggesting that you are a duffer for the most part and a chronic alcoholic for the rest.

Even if you are shooting well, it is no defence. When you have just nailed a serious archangel, he will ask loudly if you failed to see the high bird that went by above it. As you are congratulating yourself on a stonking right and left, he will announce that he has seen a shot aimed at one bird hit another before, but he has seldom seen it occur twice so close together.

And if you are drawn as a walking Gun, you need be in no doubt as to who will be strolling up the edge of the wood next to you. "Not too fast through here then, lads. If we tire him out too early on, he may never shoot anything at all. Har. Har. Har. Coming left! Oops! Were we not ready there, Sir? Har. Har. Har." As a matter of fact, this is your one chance for a modest revenge. If the gods are on your side, and the birds are feeling co-operative, there will be a steady stream of opportunities for you. Clear the mind. Focus on the birds. And carry plenty of cartridges. Pass the first one to him as you pick it up. Deliver the second brace with a wry smile. Ask him to pick the next two or three himself when he catches up with the rest of the line. Drop the first part of the next right and left just behind him when he's made it back and the second a goodly way beyond that and ask him to fetch it. From a thorn bush for choice. And then drop one on his head as he is poking about in the brambles. As the drive continues you can ask him loudly if he is managing by himself, or if he wants a boy to come and lend a hand. As he stumbles along the track in your wake, you may enquire if he wants you to wait or whether he will be arriving before the next drive. And when he does finally stagger up towards the game cart, laden with your birds and breathing hard through the stick between his teeth, you can hand him the last bird with a flourish and say quietly "Well, we seem to have scrambled one down there, don't we? Har. Har. Har." Well, it's a nice thought anyway.

VIRTUALLY UNREAL

He is immensely rich, of course. That's a given; and in case it's not for any reason, he reiterates the fact at regular intervals throughout the day. Immensely rich. A point that he underlines by sneering at the perfectly good, actually rather better than that, claret at lunchtime and asking everyone's opinion of the new Range Rover because he's thinking of getting one. Just for shooting obviously. Not for every day. And he's shot everywhere. Well, everywhere that's anywhere and it's mostly not all it's cracked up to be, you know. Oh yes, he's often invited because he is, after all, immensely rich. And his guns are the finest London pair, though not his best because he keeps his best for really challenging days on glamorous shoots rather than knockabouts like today which we were thinking was a bit cracking actually. Where the keepers really know their job, you understand, and you never have to wait more than a few minutes at your peg before the birds begin to show and where there is never a lean peg because they put down so many birds that even with double guns he has a job to keep up a sufficient rate of fire to maintain his average. He's surprised he wasn't on that list of the best shots in the kingdom, actually, though to be honest he is not sure that he wants to advertise the fact any more than he wants to be in the immensely rich list because, after all, anyone can read those things and he would not want to have to install any more elaborate security than he has already at his several large houses around the place, being as he is immensely rich.

And he never apologises as he casseroles some poor benighted pheasant no more than a couple of feet above your head. And he never even blushes as he peppers one neighbour or another swinging after a hedgehopper through the line and he never picks up the remains of the many birds he has killed at close range because that is what the pickers up are for and

he is, in any case, too immensely rich actually to carry something as ordinary as a dead pheasant. And he can't stand shooting in the rain and would rather sit out a drive in the dry of his, admittedly last year's, Range Rover than subject himself to a smattering. Well, he wouldn't mind if there were more birds to shoot at, but they clearly don't realise here what a busy man he is and not to be trifled with because at this rate they will never make the bag he was led to expect and that keeper can whistle for his tip unless he gets his act together by teatime. Torrential overnight rain, savage frost, brilliant sunshine, howling gale – just the same old excuses, you mark his words, from a keeper who doesn't know what it is to work for a living like someone who is immensely rich. Well, someone had better try to get the numbers up, he supposes, and embarks on another low level massacre while ignoring resolutely some spectacular late season rocketers which would test the best even if they didn't swell the bag by many but which might undermine his average, which is immensely good, you know.

He wants his birds, he wants his bag, he wants his Haut Brion. He wants the right peg, on the right drive, on the right day, in perfect conditions and he wants it all now or he will know the reason why and then refuse to pay up his share of the cost and undertip the keeper out of spite. If there is any justice, and we have the nerve to apply it, he will end up shooting alone in a plug in and play arcade machine which creates for him a virtual world where the countryside, the weather, the keeper, the pegs, the birds, the lunch, the tip and, critically, the friends in the line, are all figments of some melancholy micro-technology which guarantees satisfaction on an unlimited basis in exchange for a bagful of pennies. And the rest of us would be immensely pleased.

THE DANGEROUS SHOT

From the moment he exits the car, which he has parked so as to block in the game cart, you know that he is a nightmare in knicker-bockers. Even as he puts the gun together the muzzles are swinging round and about at navel level and as he attaches the sprightly springer to his cartridge belt with a long cord you realise that the full horror knows no bounds.

How he has reached this point there is no knowing. Perhaps he was never taught properly in the first place. Maybe his age and status in other parts of life have protected him, for some reason, from the proper reproofs, dressing downs and simple bawling outs which might have exorcised the demons at an earlier and less entrenched stage. But now the monster is complete and the innocent within irrecoverable.

He has no slip, sleeve or cover for his gun which is carted from drive to drive either at the trail, pointing at the knees of those in front, or balanced on his shoulder, triggers down, so that those behind are confronted by the menace of his bores. He never opens it, in either event. What he does do though is to clamp it periodically in the crook of one elbow or other while he hauls at the sprightly springer which has wrapped itself round legs of others and himself. As he whirls about to undo the resultant tangle those muzzles are circling too, addressing an eye here, a shoulder there and the napes of those who have turned away aghast.

And this is before we have even reached the pegs. Once there he extracts the woolly oil mop from the chamber of his choke barrel commenting that he has been looking for that for ages. It is replaced by cartridges. Once comprehensively loaded he cradles the piece across his chest, changing side from time to time in order to give both his neighbours equal opportunity to stare down those black holes.

When the birds put in an appearance the thing is almost unwatchable. Ignoring anything at a respectable height, he addresses those birds which hop the hedge behind which the beaters are approaching. As he focuses gimlet eyes on his chosen target the springer gathers itself to earn its title. As the bird skims the furze the dog launches itself into the retrieve as the owner slips off the safety catch. The dog reaches the end of its string as the Gun reaches the climax of his swing. Both dog and man end up flat on their backs in the mud. The bird passes unscathed, but as shocked as anyone and the shot goes....who knows? Off. Away. Somewhere. A better place. With one knee and one hand still on the sod he tries to get off a second barrel at the departing quarry so that the pickers up are not left out of the proceedings, but he is frustrated once more by the spaniel which is now seeking to make amends for its behaviour by trying to lick the mud from master's face. Roaring at the dog he hefts to his feet and straightens his belt. Ignoring the tuft of grass which now sprouts from his muzzles he reloads and settles down once more. Then spotting the possible obstruction he sticks a finger down the sharp end and wiggles it about. Then he rests the butt on his boot, as the springer gambols, and squints down the tubes to make sure they are clear of turf. Reassured, he once more assumes the ready position. It is not yet 10 o'clock. He rummages in his pocket for his flask. Faint. Feign a coronary. Food poisoning. Galloping dysentery. Divorce. Anything. Get out. Go home. Save yourself. All the pheasants ever bred. Especially if it's you.

THE HOST'S WIFE

Dear God, will the shooting season never end? Snatch an early coffee before facing the horrors. First job is to light the fires in the hall and the dining room in order to take the chill off from the draughts which whistle around these forgotten corners of the house during the winter months. Then the horses have to be fed and the dogs have to be given a run and then their breakfast so that they are fettled for the day's work. Stoke up the fires and fill all the log baskets and start breakfast. Coffee on. Porridge onto the Aga, bacon and sausages into the slow oven. Get the soup and sausage rolls for elevenses from the freezer and stick them on the draining board before venturing upstairs to rouse the children. Grab the old man's stockings from in front of the stove and hurl them at him as you pass. "Darling, where the hell are my stock…thank you!" The procedure might be carved in stone. Kids washed and clothed, back downstairs to empty the dishwasher onto the breakfast table, break out the bread, butter, marmalade and OJ, check the porridge, take the coffee off, refill the kettle and move the cooked breakfast from the slow oven to the fast. A quick peek outside the backdoor to see the keeper and a couple of the stops backing the beater's wagon onto the hitch, so back into the kitchen to make large pot of tea and first round of bacon sarnies for them. Call upstairs to see whether husband remembered to fill the Land Rover with diesel last night and listen with grim satisfaction to the tirade that inevitably flows back. Pour tea and create bacon sarnies and open back door just as the keeper's finger is approaching the knocker. "He'll be down in twenty. Can you juice up the Landy. He's forgotten again!" "Twenty it is. Very good, missus. Already done it. " Back into the kitchen, dole out porridge. "It's on the table!" Swig coffee. It's just gone 8.00am. Into the dining room. Make up the fire and lay the table for fourteen for lunch. Give the silver a buff and knock the corks off six bottles of claret and stick them on the mantelpiece to breathe. Decant two bottles of port. Make up hall fire on way back into the kitchen. "Darling, have you seen the cards? I think they…." "On the table in the hall with your cartridge belt." Soup off the draining board and into the slow oven. Thermoses out of the pantry. Kids out of the kitchen and into the scullery. Boots, coats, hats, gloves, leggings, sticks. "Right. You're done. Do as you are told and have a good day!" "Darling? Dog leads?" "Hanging by the back door." Pastry out of the fridge, steak and kidney out of the pantry. Check the drinks basket – sloe gin, damson brandy, vodka and sherry for the soup. Glasses. Yes. Cups. Cups? Bugger! Cups? Cups already the basket in the back of the Landy. Into the kitchen. Clear breakfast table. "Darling, where is my cap?" "You're wearing it." "Ah!" "Right. Set? I'll see you at the Piggeries at 11.00 for drinks and soup and sausage rolls. Lunch for fourteen will be on the table here at 1.00 and tea will be ready at 4.00. Gamedealer's due at 5.00 OK? OK. Go get 'em Tiger! Mwah!"

So that's just the veggies to peel, two horses to exercise, puddings to defrost, the steak and kidney to finish, the VAT return to post, bathe and beautify, pick up two of the Guns' wives at the pub in the village in order to be at the Piggeries in two hours flat looking drop dead gorgeous, relaxed and glamorous enough to charm the socks off all and sundry and get back here in time to make up the fires, dish up the lunch and still be entertaining. Then bake two cakes for tea. And the baby sitter to pick up because they have to be out at dinner by eight. Multi-tasking? Means nothing to me, poppet, just another day at the office. Dear God, will the shooting season never end?

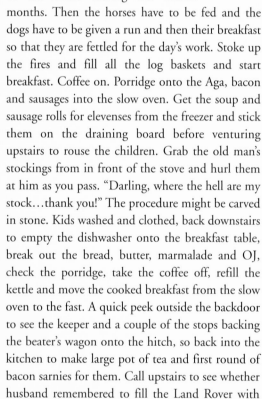

THE UNDOMESTIC GODDESS

From the moment she jumps out of her natty little hatchback the assembled company is duly polarized. The men are agog and the women are aghast. For there are men's men and girl's girls. And then there is this, a man's girl. From the tumbling blond scruff cut which frames baby blues and peaches and cream at one end to the split deer-hide suede breeks at the other and everything else that is tightly packed in between she is every bachelor's dream and every girlfriend's nightmare. The legend down the side of her stockings – "Your bird, Sir!" does nothing for anyone's nerves.

And as she puts together the sweetest little Gardone 20 bore, which was a birthday present from some admirer, all eyes are on her. And as she empties a last box of Rottweilers into her cartridge bag and turns to meet the Guns there is a degree of foot shuffling and general harrumphing. And so she is introduced around by her mischievous host, who knows full well the impact she is having. And she shakes hands and looks candidly and modestly around as the other ladies and gentlemen find themselves struggling with, Ah, conflicting emotions. The men want to fling her into the nearest haybarn and the girls into the nearest water trough.

And the truth is, she doesn't care. She comes not to flirt but to shoot; which she does, as a matter of fact, extremely well. The youngest sibling following a stream of hulking great sons, and an afterthought at that, she was the apple of her Father's eye. And while he indulged her disgracefully, his indulgence was limited to those areas with which he was familiar. And so she shoots, extremely tidily; and she can lay a good long line and light with a fifteen-foot double hander or a chalk stream wand with equal facility; and she's no slouch with a rifle either, on the hill or the ranges. It is just an accident of fate that at the same time as she snatches salmon from their pools or nails a tall cockbird going back across the corner of the wood, there are men in the vicinity sighing deeply and declaring that their tiny hearts are breaking. While variously their wives, girlfriends, spouses, partners and mothers tell them in no uncertain terms to pull themselves together and get on with the job in hand.

And the irony of the whole seething situation is that when it is she who finds herself confronted by some custom built, hand stitched, drop dead dreamboat who renders her weak at the knees with suppressed passion, she blushes furiously and can't think of anything sensible to say. There is justice.

THE BELTED EARL

Also known to his inmates as 'the Belting Earl' on account of his habit of belting birds at prodigious distances which have dodged his neighbour's neighbour's gun. He never practices because, what with his own moor behind one castle and the sumptuous pheasant shoot in front of the other, he scarcely has the time. And that is before the invitations. With five days on the driving moor and the schedule in the park he issues a fair old stack of shooting invites himself every season and notwithstanding the numbers of relatives and business guests upon whom he bestows them, several dozen guests are likely to invite him back. Most of these are other belted earls, so that the season is a long round of moated manors and battlemented castles and sundry assorted gamebirds scudding, flaring and soaring as the season and species require.

He manages to shoot both diffidently and well. In between the highest and fastest and apologetically 'tidying up' behind – a long way behind – most of the rest of the line, he spends much of the time on his peg arguing with the scruffy dogs who accompany him everywhere and which tend to be the result of an unguarded moment between the castle kennels and a passing stranger of indeterminate parentage who accompanied the man who came to mend the roof of the west wing. The Countess, whose hobby is the careful and selected breeding and training of peerless retrievers was naturally mortified, but the Belted Earl took a fancy to the offspring, and promptly adopted one as his personal mascot. In a couple of generations the Labshund or the Terraniel will be a must-have fashion accessory among Hello! Readers. The family motto ('Suffer the Lowly') may be variously interpreted as welcoming scruffy dogs onto the sofa of the Chinese Velvet Drawing Room, or having to put up with the coach-loads of tourists who spend the summer traipsing round whichever the castle the Belted Earl is not presently inhabiting. So the estates wash their collective faces and the tourists keep the castles roofed and wired, which leaves the Belted Earl free to sit on the board of sundry companies which make useful investments in software companies in California, where a title opens more doors than you could shake a coronet at, which periodically float at shocking subscription levels, leaving the Belted Earl as surprised as anyone but considerably richer than most. And which allows him to shoot most days during the season, which is why he shoots so well, and how he became known as the Belting Earl, which is where we came in.

THE WIFE'S DOG

He is Wolfie. He is master of all he surveys and he answers to no one. He is locked and loaded and ready to howl. He is top dog. Numero Uno. The Wolfie.

Wolfie is a small, round, sort of Cairn, maybe Yorkshire, perhaps Patterdale, partly at least Jack Russell, terrier. Wolfie is the apple of his Mama's eye and gets away with murder. He chews everything he can reach. Except for those things, those expensive things, which have been purchased on his behalf and for his exclusive use as things to be chewed. These he eschews and scorns utterly. Instead he buries them down the back of the sofas in the drawing room. And gives the loose covers a bit of a chew. And disembowels a cushion. And pees on the standard lamp. Which was recently bought to cover up the yellow patch on the Wilton from the last time that Wolfie visited parts foreign. Now the standard lamp will have to become a prayer mat. And in due season, probably a runner; then a rug, until finally a compromise is reached whereby Wolfie is no longer barred from the drawing room, at which point he will no longer pee and no longer chew. Not there, anyway. There are other rooms he has his eye on still. Not that life below stairs is altogether uncomfortable. He has a basket in the kitchen, obviously; but on the whole he prefers the sitting room. He has a basket there too, but he prefers the sofa. Only when there's company though. People he can growl at with rolling eyes and bared fangs. When he's alone he sits on Mama's chair because it carries her scent which comforts him through all the long minutes he is alone between meals.

And on shoot days Wolfie accompanies his mistress who accompanies the bloke who loiters about the house at weekends in the summer, but who appears to have no function flat. First Wolfie picks a fight with the biggest and ugliest of the Labradors he meets upon bouncing out of the car. This sometimes takes a bit of doing because the Labradors all seem to have other things on their minds, but once Wolfie has sniffed their bottoms, butted their muzzles and humped them from one end of the gravel to the other one of them usually cracks whereupon Wolfie runs howling to his Mama's ankles and stands there grinning which duly establishes his place in the pecking order for the day which is in the shadow of the Alpha female which is as good as a force field and twice as powerful.

On the peg he watches and whimpers with excitement as birds fall about him. But even Wolfie knows that he is not a retriever. He has no interest in dead pheasants and less still in lugging them about. Leave that for the dumb Labradors. Wolfie has better sport in mind. And his moment comes when the bloke who loiters about the house says "Bugger!" and a pheasant tumbles not pell-mell but lands running. That's for Wolfie. He's off like a train, legs going like pistons. He barks as he runs because this will encourage the pheasant to make an effort and prolong the whole jaunt. He howls as he body-slams the old cock. He yips as he kills it with a sharp crunch of jaws pumped to muscular perfection on a thousand marrow bones and the legs of several rather nice, once, pre Wolfie, dining chairs. And then, because he can, he grabs the remains by one leg and drags the cadaver across the grass towards Mama. Who is not mad keen on dead pheasants, it must be said, even if delivered by Wolfie, but for her Wolfie no praise is too great. "Ooh! 'Oooos a clever Wolfie dog, then? Izzen 'e a clever boy den? You see, darling, he retrieved it all by himself. Oooooooh! Aren't you jus' the clev'rest 'iddle Wolfie baby?" And Wolfie sits once more and licks the blood of his muzzle. He is No.1. The Wolf-dog. Yeah!

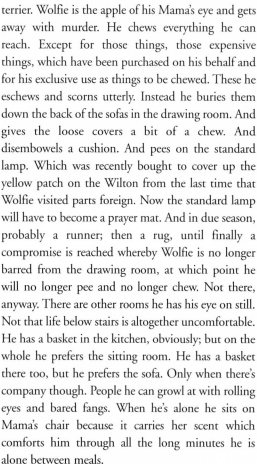

THE FARMER

You come across him, generally speaking, not far from home. As it might be Lincs perhaps, or somewhere out in the Fens down Cambridge way; maybe Yorkshire. But wherever you encounter him the chances are that the pheasants are well known to be very, very good and the claret is quietly recognized as being some of the best going and not stuck to the bottle either. And there he sits on his shooting stick, feet well spread and an abundant girth comfortably settled in between. Collar adrift and gloveless for all it's just about zero degrees. A pipe smoulders comfortably from the corner of his mouth and the gun rests easily in the crook of one elbow. Hands the size of ploughshares on his knees as hooded blue eyes scan the distant wood for the first of the birds. This is a man at ease with himself and his environment. Ruddy of face and whiskered of chin he may be, but this is no yeoman son of soil and toil. Four thousand acres of prime arable and every inch of it managed to within an inch of its life. He's always worked hard and played hard and he will be damned if anything about him will get away with doing any less. Then there are the holiday cottages and the 4x4 circuits and the cross country course which represent a diversified revenue stream as well as finding something to do with the old barns on the one hand and the thoroughly shagged out set-aside on the other. He doesn't shoot at home because the pheasants are just too damned easy. Besides which there are rich City bond traders who are more than happy to pay him well over the odds to shoot them while he takes himself off after something halfway respectable. And when something halfway respectable does put in an appearance, starling sized, archangel height and going like the proverbial clappers he seems scarcely to notice it until it is almost upon him whereupon the old Purdey is hefted up in a twinkling, like a wand in those great paws, and the next thing there is the bird bouncing to a definitive halt right behind his peg and he is back in the same position of relaxed repose. Three days a week in the season, old partner, for more seasons than you can shake a stick at, man and boy, and never had a lesson in his life.

THE HIGH PHEASANT SPECIALIST

Thirty-four-inch barrels, ported by Mag-Na-Port. Full and full, natch. Monte Carlo stock and single trigger, of course, and the whole thing weighs nearer eight pounds than seven. Basically a trap gun with a comb so high it'll have your eye out; for all it is handcrafted in Gardone by the finest Italian craftsmen and costs a small, scratch that, a large fortune. Slap a 'scope on the top and it would be a rifle. But when you are shoving $1\frac{1}{4}$ oz of nickel-plated Hi-Powa Dynamite Dobermanns in the other end you need some bulk to absorb the repercussions when the action starts. Try a couple of boxes of these total headbangers yourself in short order when you have half an hour to spare and suddenly the slightly vacant and faraway expression of the High-Pheasant Specialist begins to make sense.

And what is the objective of this pain and anguish? To shoot pheasants which are a very long way away indeed. Not fast pheasants necessarily, like they have out on the Fens, or the wild unruly pheasants that hurtle cackling from the bracken beds of East Anglia or corkscrew through the branches of the hanging woods of Yorkshire. No. These are perfectly ordinary pheasants launched off vertiginous escarpments which plummet towards the distant valley floor where, like an ant at the foot of a dry well, stands the High-Pheasant Specialist. The drives are called K2, or Cumulo Nimbus or perhaps the Outer Rings of Saturn. Like cars called The Senator or Grande Luxe or Tankbuster, the names seek by inference to raise the perceived quality of these unfortunate birds to somewhere above and beyond the mere quarry that the rest of us pursue. And to justify the truly sky-high amounts of money with which the High-Pheasant Specialist parts in order to let off his gun many times down a deep hole.

There once was a man who stood in his garden in the heart of the city and let off his gun many times. A policeman arrived and enquired of the citizen what he was about. 'I'm shooting the famous high pheasants of the West Country,' said he, 'It's rare sport and no mistake.' The bobby scratched his bonce, bemused; 'But we are hundreds of miles from the West Country.' 'Aye.' said the shooter, with a wink, 'they may not actually be very high, but they surely are a bloody long way away!'

THE HEAD KEEPER

He bunked off school aged nine and three quarters to collect eggs for the headkeeper's bantams when the Euston System was an innovation. After being routinely thrashed by teacher and parents he variously decked the one and left the other to become deputy assistant apprentice to the junior deputy under-keeper on an outlying beat of the estate just before the war. Exactly which war is an issue into which it is best not to probe too deeply, but the odds are that it involved red tunics and the rapid formation of squares. After which, the bulk of the keepering staff having been wiped out, he was promoted to beat-keeper by the present owner's grandfather - "the Major" - and received the princely wage of six shillings a week, a cottage, a new suit and a bucket of beer on quarter-days.

Following his single handed destruction of a gang of poachers with a tent-peg, a ball of string and his fists, his talents were recognised and on the retirement of the legendary head keeper Jack "Rabbit" Skinner shortly after the next war, he was made headkeeper by the then young "Colonel".

Much has changed, of course, but certain principles yet hold. Despite being as old as the hills, he will still confront any "Gyppos and Diddicoys" who venture onto the estate and establish their obedience to his supremacy by giving the headman a good kicking. He goes on poacher patrol nightly and while he leans more heavily on his stick than once he did, it is as feared in the vicinity as the tent-peg ever was. He still consumes his bucket of beer at regular intervals and if you can catch him in the mood after it, he will share with you the secrets of running a successful shoot, how to rear partridges against the odds and how to make a pheasant fly through the eye of a needle. Add another pint and he'll tell you why he has been happily married for five decades or more, how to charm a fox to within stroking distance and the real reason why a visiting Gun sent him a pair of Purdey sidelocks as a gesture of appreciation.

On shoot days he is immediately identifiable by the shininess of his boots, the cut of his suit and his trademark stiff collar. His manoeuvres, all of which are recorded in a notebook and rehearsed at length with the boss, key stops and flankers the evening before a shoot day, take into account wind direction, sun, topography, date, air temperature, ground temperature, and above all his opinion of the Guns. Each drive is well practised and executed with a minimum of noise except for the steady tap-tap-tap of the beaters' sticks. His days are always successful. Some are great, but none fail. He does not expect to be tipped, but accepts such offerings as the Guns tender. On one notable occasion, however, after a pheasant day that could only be described as spectacular, he was moved to comment. Without so much as a glance at the tip he had received as he handed a visiting Gun his brace, and which he could feel was as inadequate for the quality of the day as the Gun's shooting had been, he held out his closed fist and pressed the contents back into the miscreant's hand announcing loudly "If that's your idea of gratitude, young man, I'll settle for respect." Which is as it should be.

THE ROCK STAR

"Well, I was born a thousand years ago, with a guitar in my hand. I was busted out of school, y'know, an' then I joined the band……..DODGER STADIUM!!! HOW Y'ALL DOIN' OUT THERE???????" or as it might be London or Rio or Shanghai or Sydney or Reykyavik for that matter. Sing the same songs, play the same tunes, burn up the fret board, trash the occasional hotel room, get busted now and then, get drunk a good deal, and get laid by wannabe supermodels with one eye on the paparazzi from Bootle to Bombay and back again; pick up the cheque at the end of the tour and hightail it back to the farmhouse in the deepest part of the remotest village in rural England, chill out, detox, walk the dogs, go shooting.

The rural rocker tends to roll up to charity shoots in a Saab with a knock-out girl in the passenger seat. It's about as anonymous as you can get. For a light supper in the West End, at Caprice or the Ivy or Nobu, the blacked out Range Rover is virtually de rigeur and on shooting days, of course, he poles along in a venerable Defender pick-up with a canvas back, the spare tyre on the front for putting pheasants in and a bakelite steering wheel. But for the charity shoot where there isn't, after all, going to be any great mud-plugging between drives, he favours the Saab. Nor is there any sign of the flamboyant stage persona so beloved of headbanging, lighter-waving, air-guitaring, larynx bursting fans around the globe. The spray-on snakeskin trews and the PVC singlet are notable only by their absence. The traditional headband and aviator shades are missing and neither silken scarves nor a hundredweight of chain adorn his wrists. Instead he clambers from the driving seat dapper in lightweight tweed breeks and waistcoat, tattersall checks and desert boots. The standard garb, in fact, for the multimillion album selling, drug crazed, leather lunged, rock and roll revolutionary in this part of the county. The teams today are four apiece and his crew includes the drummer from the band who has motored over for the weekend from his place near Oxford with his wife and the quartet is made up by the superstar's teenage daughter, the looker from the car, who is more often to be seen moving steadily up the three-day event rankings but who shoots very tidily as well and is always ready to turn out with her old dad and her trusty twenty.

The day follows a well ordered procedure and as the superstar and his team make their way round the different stands there is a deal of joshing from the scorers and trappers and the other Guns, many of whom are old friends more or less evenly drawn from the shooting field, the local county set, stage and screen, large and small, and the international rock and roll circus on its day off. "Lucky that's not being amplified to 80,000 impressionable teenagers, matey!" says the scorer as the heavy metal riff king mutters a curse or three after a missed pair. "Still, not to worry. Two more to come. That's better. See? Bit of ginger driving the swing there, eh? Rock and roll, then old mate. Catch you in the tent after?" And at the barbecue lunch later there are enough stars assembled that one out of uniform rocker can blend in without a second thought. He buys a nice sounding day's shooting at a bargain price in the auction and then overbids outrageously for an autographed copy of one of his own albums to much laughter and applause as he is finally loudly identified by the auctioneer.

Then it is back into the Saab for the short journey back to the farm in time to walk the dogs and review the dates for the next global mega-tour.

THE DUFFER

He's prompt. He's smart. He's tremendously good company; and he's completely safe. Even the pheasants have no worries on that score because he just can't hit anything. He has a perfectly ordinary gun; he has the same cartridges as everybody else; he even has a fairly reasonable, if somewhat frustrated, dog; he just can't hit anything.

He joined the team several seasons gone. He had been floating about on the periphery for some little while and when he heard there was a slot going spare, well, he was just mustard. The captain interviewed him and he seemed reasonable enough, and jolly company to boot, and he never flinched when told the sub. But when he turned up on the first day, he just couldn't hit anything.

He doesn't shoot the beaters and he never gives the other Guns a moment's pause; he just doesn't hit anything. At all. He won't shoot low birds. There are those who rather wish he would because everyone knows he's never going to touch the high ones; he misses them by miles, and there is a subdued groan from the field every time another sparkling bouquet veers inevitably in his direction to no discernible effect. He never harms a feather. He just can't hit anything.

His undiminished good humour and his evident enjoyment of the day serve only to underline his astonishing incompetence. He isn't old or disabled or blinking behind bottle bottom goggles; he just can't hit anything. The skipper resolutely fixes the draw to put him between a couple of top Guns and his neighbours do what they can to cover the gap in the line, but they can't, or won't, kill everything he lets by, and despite the fact that his total lack of contribution means more fun and frolics for the other Guns, everyone finds themselves wishing that he could just shoot something. Occasionally. Or once. For the dog's peace of mind, if nothing else.

There was a moment where he was in the hottest of hot seats and there were birds zooming in all directions. His neighbours did sterling work and there were birds dropping left, right and centre and plenty more to come. It just seemed inconceivable that he could get lead in the air without connecting with something. A pheasant did collapse at one point which everyone said must be his, but he resolutely denied any knowledge of it and claimed to be aiming elsewhere at the time. No-one had the heart to tell him that was why they thought he might have shot it.

But he's happy and relaxed and charming and funny and prompt and smart and safe. He just can't hit anything.

BOXING DAY

On the one hand the young Guns are all agog with eagerness and anticipation. They have been looking forward to this ever since their qualifying birthday. "When you are twelve…" or as it might be "This year…..", "Next year……." Whatever. The fact is that today is Boxing Day and this is, categorically, definitively and absolutely IT. The day. The first day. The first shooting day. With a gun and cartridges and beaters and everything. With grown-ups. The new cartridge belt has been worn overnight and loaded since dawn. The gun has been cleaned to within an inch of its life and is in its new sleeve. Boots are clean, trousers pressed, hands washed, hair brushed. Six months of good, goodish behaviour and a cracking set of exam results have gone into today and nothing can stop it now. Pleeeease!

For the grown-ups the perception is somewhat different. First there is the sleep deprivation. You cannot, after all, do stockings effectively until all the children are asleep. Which on Christmas Eve is late, late, late. Then again Christmas morn breaks earlier than any but the most savage working day. "Look, I got a fire engine. It goes WAH-WAH-WAH!!!" "Don't feed those to the dog. It will make her ….. Well, what do you mean she already has? Where?"

Then, of course, there was the gargantuan gluttony of yesterday, which just went on and on and on. It is true that if you cannot knock the neck off that special bottle of extra, super, de luxe V.V.V.S.O.P cognac at Christmas, then when can you? And it was everything it said in the explanatory leaflet that came in the ornately sealed and ribboned box. But was it really sensible to lower it quite as far as we did? On top of the port and the Stilton and the mince pies and the Turkish Delight and the crystallised ginger?

And when was the last time you smoked a cigar quite that enormous? And lived? On top of all this there are the new socks to remember to wear. The silly hat to retrieve from the back of the wardrobe. Lunch to pack – "It's your turn today, matey. Where'd you think all that stuff yesterday came from? Out of a tin?" Dogs to exercise, guns to find, gloves, boots, sticks. A box of cartridges. Yes, and yours. Yes, and theirs. Wars have been fought with less equipment.

The girls, of course, are offensively chipper. It's their day off, the first and only, after weeks of unremitting toil and in-laws and outlaws and drinks parties and office parties and carol concerts and pantomimes and worse. They also have their new boots and fur waistcoats to contrast and compare as well as that extra special little present that lurks at the toe of the stocking and which should never be less than several carats. Not if you want to shoot on Boxing Day, anyway. And they have their 20 bores sleeved and ready too.

For the keeper it's another day at the office. There was a short break yesterday between the morning's dogging-in, pegging out today's drives, the afternoon feed and cleaning down the game larder when he and the missus, who had been plucking a dozen brace or so for the Guns today, enjoyed a glass and a cracker and exchanged gifts. But this is his time and tomorrow is as much an important day as any great battue of the season. More, Boxing Day is a gift from keepers to a new generation, a new line of Guns for the years to come. New shooting tenants, new bosses perhaps. For better or worse, more work. Another day at the office. Old Gun or Young Gun you should remember that when you shake the keeper's hand on Boxing Day.

THE TACKLE MONSTER

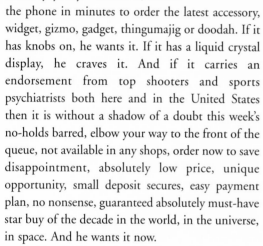

He is the equipment ogre, the gear giant, the kit kraken. He is the Tackle Monster. Thumbing through every new issue of every known magazine whether weekly, monthly, yearly – whenever, he's on the phone in minutes to order the latest accessory, widget, gizmo, gadget, thingumajig or doodah. If it has knobs on, he wants it. If it has a liquid crystal display, he craves it. And if it carries an endorsement from top shooters and sports psychiatrists both here and in the United States then it is without a shadow of a doubt this week's no-holds barred, elbow your way to the front of the queue, not available in any shops, order now to save disappointment, absolutely low price, unique opportunity, small deposit secures, easy payment plan, no nonsense, guaranteed absolutely must-have star buy of the decade in the world, in the universe, in space. And he wants it now.

He has cartridge bags of every material, shade, hue and colour. And a camouflage one too. He has belts and bandoliers and magazines, ancient and modern, in harness leather and brass corners. He has dispensers and speed-loaders and re-loaders and lead and steel and tungsten and bismuth and tin and molybdenum and magnum and hi-power and lo-recoil and smokeless and smell-less and probably shotless and bang-less too. Pointless he has in abundance. And he has lightweight clothes and heavyweight suits and matching hats and co-ordinated sets. And he has them in estate tweed, spring green, broken pattern, quick dry, waterproof, medium twill, autumn shade, heat reflecting, breathable, winter warmer, ergonomic, flexi-shoulder, high waist, low maintenance, self cleaning, stay pressed and elastic as well as standard khaki drab, obviously. He has a kilt.

He has decoys, flappers, lofters, tweeters, magnets and southerns which variously squeak, coo, flop, flit, fly, bob, quack and dawdle. And don't even get him started on his boots. Lace up, zip up, buckle up and velcro. Leather, rubber, suede, neoprene and sheepskin and then there's the insides still to come. Studded, ribbed, commando or hobnailed and, yes, we are still on boots. For now.

Should we, dare we, mention the gun cupboard? Long barrels and short. Side by side and over and under. Trap, skeet, field and game. Straight hand, half pistol, Prince of Wales, full pistol, Monte Carlo, thumbhole. Clip on cheek pieces and stock extensions. Comb raisers and high visibility fluorescent foresight beads. In red, yellow and orange depending on the time of year, day of the week, time of day and which colour glasses you are wearing. Nylon slips, canvas slips, leather cover. Buckle and zip. Handle and strap.

And the Game Fair is just about heaven and hell both for him, because there is everything here on display at once in a full range of models and colours each with handy matching travelling sac and a full set of attachments and try as he might there isn't enough time in three days to see everything and to test, review, try out, compare and contrast all the stuff on offer nor indeed is there enough money in the Bank of England to buy it all even if his credit card had not already melted from the strain. So it is just possible that the Tackle Monster might get spending exhaustion before he's even got to the end of Gunmaker's Row which would be a pity because watching him make a stately and increasingly carrierbagged progression down Fisherman's Row is something of an annual institution since down there they really know about how to reel in a Tackle Monster.